THE SOLDIER BOY

Bob Freeman

was

THE SOLDIER BOY

With a Foreword
by
Lt. Col. (M.A.A.) V.K. Freeman
Late Army Physical Training Corps

GEORGE MANN *of* MAIDSTONE

Bob Freeman

was

THE SOLDIER BOY

Copyright © Robert Bruce Freeman, 1996

Robert Bruce Freeman has asserted his right under Section 77
of the Copyright, Designs and Patents Act 1988 to be
identified as the author
of this book

First published 1996, by George Mann Books

ISBN 0 7041 0262 5

Printed and bound in
the United Kingdom by
Longdunn Press Ltd, Bristol
and published by
George Mann Books
in the English County of Kent

THE SOLDIER BOY

Foreword

by Lt. Col. (M.A.A.) V.K. Freeman
Late Army Physical Training Corps

There have been many books written about the pageantry, pomp and privilege of the British Raj, but few indeed in this century about the life of the ordinary trooper in India, and that of his children. At last, we now see the other, less glamorous side of the British Cavalry Regiments supporting "The Jewel in the Crown".

In this book, my brother paints a picture of those behind the barrack gates—especially the children who were dragged round the world from one posting to another, with frequent changes of accommodation, life-styles and often inadequate schools. For me, it is a tribute to my mother and all Service wives who, though rated by officialdom as being of secondary importance to the Army and its Regiments, suffered in silence, supported their husbands and families and were a constant source of compassion and love.

When my father's regiment, the 16th/5th Queen's Royal Lancers, moved to India in 1937, we left England's shores with few regrets but our new home provoked other feelings. We soon realised that an Army Cantonment in India was a world of its own with its own hierarchy, rules and order of precedence. The requirements of the Regiment and the horses were always given first priority, and the welfare of troopers' families was way down the list, with children mostly just tolerated and certainly not allowed to get in the way of Army routine or camp life.

With my father constantly absent on duty and my mother pregnant with sister Pauline, my brothers and I were left in the care of ayahs and to our own devices. My father, a strict disciplinarian, made it clear that, as the eldest, I was responsible for the safety and behaviour of my brothers. Bob, the next oldest, had ideas of his own. Trouble with local traders, complaints from tonga wallahs,

1

and going missing for hours in the local bazaar, often without his topee, brought swift punishment from my father, but Bob's rebel spirit could not be tamed.

After a year, we moved to the North West Frontier and my father became almost a stranger to us, out on patrol for long periods in the never-ending conflict against Pathan tribesmen who attempted frequent murderous forays from their mountain strongpoints in the Himalayas on to the plains below. During these long absences, my mother—whose patience, love and generosity was unfailing—had to manage as best she could and she was always there for us.

The outbreak of the Second World War saw the Regiment recalled to England where, within only four weeks, my mother was deserted again when my father was sent to America. A traumatic period followed with more moves for my mother to put up with and—worse, much worse—the tragic loss of two of her sons, my two youngest brothers, within one month of each other. Under this burden my mother's health broke and the family had to split up. Brother Bob was banished to the Duke of York's Royal Military School and, oddly enough after all the years of conflict between us, I missed him. He achieved a sort of infamy in the school's history yet, reading this book, one can perhaps understand why.

In my father's last years as a Chelsea Pensioner, he recorded his thoughts for posterity and referred to Bob as the awkward one of his brood. I think this book proves him right. Nevertheless, I am proud that my brother has lifted the edge of the curtain on some long gone, fascinating and often moving memorable times.

1

LOOKING BACK it seems appropriate that I started life in great pain; that I was at fault; that I was insignificant, a pawn on life's chessboard. It set a pattern and that pattern remains.

The pain was not that first slap on the arse, we've all had that. No, it was some years later when we first start laying down those vivid childhood memories we will always recall.

I remember that polo ball well. It was speeding towards me but I stood mesmerised.

I didn't feel its impact to start with; there was a "crack" and I was flat on my back.

A sea of faces looked down on me and horses' heads were puffing smoke behind them. Walrus-face with his huge nicotine-stained moustache was still speaking as he bent forward and looked down at me; the red veins all over his fat face and his red bulbous nose intrigued me.

They put me in a car; I'd never been in a car before. It had wooden beams criss-crossed on the outside and two doors at the back. There was an Alsatian dog behind the back seat; its wagging tail kept hitting the window.

I was quite excited, my first time in a car, and, all my pals watching, green with envy—me in an officer's car.

They all stood staring, as the officers talked, polo ponies all round. I couldn't see my brother Vic anywhere.

Someone had fetched my Dad from the stables.

'Sorry, Freeman, caught your boy with a polo ball, standing a bit too close to goal, told them before, you know,' said the walrus. 'Must get him off to hospital. Broken ankle, I think. You go with him—Fanshawe will drive.'

'Yes, sir,' said Father, coming rigidly to attention.

'Let me know how things are, Freeman,' said Fatty as he remounted his quivering pony.

3

'Soon as I get back, sir.'

You knew your place in the cavalry and if you were a trooper it wasn't hard to remember—bottom of the pile; you always looked up.

Dad slipped into the back seat having first eased my legs off the shiny leather.

'Don't put your shoes on the officers' seat son.'

'No Dad.'

'Sit up—we'll soon be there.'

My leg was hurting like hot hammers were pounding inside it, but I tried not to cry.

We had been marching with the band, just like real soldiers, just like our Dads. It had been just another normal day.

The band practised most days, usually around the army camp roads and no-one took much notice of us ragged "soldiers" marching out of step, swinging our arms ridiculously high, laughing and enjoying every minute.

The tarmac on the road was bubbling, breaking through the surface, shiny and beautifully black. It stuck to our dirty sandals as we enjoyed the sensation of deliberately stepping on the little volcanoes and prising our feet away. The heat haze shimmered about two feet above the camp road; I could see it, but when I got closer it had gone, moved forward another twenty feet; it was like chasing a rainbow.

We stood on the road by the stables. We could see across the sixty yards of grass, edged all round by the camp road, the communal clothes lines hanging heavy with washing outside the blocks of married quarters.

The band was stationary now as the bandmaster gave yet another lecture to the sweating bandsmen. The poor bass-drummer, still with his leopard skin over his uniform, was losing weight by the minute.

We, the camp kids, at least twenty of us, stood looking around, talking and waiting for the band to start up, there was nothing else to do.

A few troopers were going hither and thither, dressed in their thick khaki tunics clipped up to the neck. Their puttees neatly bandaged their ankles and calves above their big black boots, ensuring no air got in to cool their hot bodies; no summer uniforms in the army—one uniform for minus two degrees or plus eighty.

A warm breeze coated us with a whiff of hay and horse dung from the stables twenty yards to the right; how I loved that smell.

The sound of horses neighing and clip-clopping across cobbled yards echoed constantly, broken by barks of command coming from the parade ground. It was August 1935, and school summer holidays.

Someone had spotted the ice-cream man and like a swarm of locusts, the little army deserted its post to land on the salesman, obliterating him from the landscape.

Pennies and halfpennies were excitedly extracted from handfuls of pocket treasures, pretty glass marbles glinting in the bright sunshine, bent cigarette cards of sleek Bentleys, half-chewed sweets stuck to bits of string, cardboard milk tops won in competition against the barrack wall.

Little arms shot out like spears, proffering coins in excited voices, tinged with the fear of hearing 'Sorry, son—sold out of them.' It had happened before.

The shiny peak-capped, white-coated Walls ice cream man stood behind the handlebars of his three-wheeled tricycle, one leg either side of the pedals, and lifted the lid of the big, square freezer box in front of him. The white dusty frost crept into the daylight from the black hole within and disappeared in the glaring hot sunshine as he searched for halfpenny orange ices. What a glorious sight as he handed out five-inch-long, triangular sticks, each covered in a snug-fitting coat of soft cardboard.

Not all the kids had money, but that didn't stop us from enjoying the excitement. Victor, my elder brother, and I, stood close to the tub but I couldn't see inside like the big kids. I'd love to see inside that tub, I thought. It was pure magic how it kept producing more and more ice-creams and all of them so hard and cold on a blazing hot day.

'Any more?' said the salesman.

I looked at Vic; he said, 'Come on,' and we walked away, following the crowd.

'Give us a lick,' I said to my best friend Jimmy Gordon.

'No—get your own!' the words blazed out through his orange coloured mouth. So much for best friends.

We ambled aimlessly across the grass between the stables and the married quarters to the sucking and the slurping of the lucky ones, and the envious sidelong glances of the penniless.

'I know,' said a penniless one, 'let's go to the polo match—we might get a penny there.'

As of one mind, the locust swarm took off and landed twenty feet behind the goal post at the stables end of the polo pitch, where the officers practised nearly every day and often threw pennies to the troopers' kids if they quickly retrieved long hit balls. Vic and I had watched them play many times, but I wasn't quick enough to earn a penny; the big boys always beat me to it. My hope was for Vic to get the ball and of course a penny; then we might just catch the Walls man before he left the camp.

All officers were expected to play polo; indeed, their career prospects depended on it. The Regiment—the 16th/5th Queen's Own Royal Lancers—was a fine cavalry regiment and, as in all cavalry regiments, life revolved around the horses. Life for an officer between the wars and especially during the 1930's, was one of horses and socialising.

The History Book of the 16th/5th, the Queen's Royal Lancers is filled page after page, year after year, with achievements of the polo team, or point-to-point race winners or, in one instance, in 1931, with the performances of a pack of beagles taken over from the Royal Scots Greys: 'They showed excellent sport.' Officers also joined the local hunts wherever the regiment moved.

Yes, life was hard for the poor officer with all that riding to do. Of course the horses and indeed the polo ponies had to be fed, brushed, exercised, and trained. Saddles, bridles, leather and brasswork had to be cleaned and polished—but all this was the job of the trooper; the backbone of the cavalry.

The troopers' sons came to love horses and as I watched the polo match my eyes were fixed with sadness on the poor little polo pony, whose neck and flanks wore a white necklace of steaming sweat. Its head was jerked back by an impetuous and impatient tight rein which made its rump drop a foot and forced its two back legs into the hard packed ground, throwing dirt and small stones to its underbelly. The pony's frightened and panic-stricken eyes attempted to look backwards at the obese walrus that was cursing obscenities as he swung his mallet right under the pony's neck. They nearly collided with the bandaged goal post and as I watched this sad spectacle, I surmised that the officer was nearly as heavy as the pony and pictured him running around, bridle to his head and the pony across his shoulders; he then might care a little for the poor beast he was nearly breaking in two.

The next thing I knew I was lying on the ground with all the officers and ponies surrounding me.

Mother glided down the shiny, brown linoleum carrying baby John. He could have walked but the floor looked slippery and other visitors were charging across it with flowers and oranges to the fore, eyes darting from left to right looking for the familiar face. Vic followed behind Mother.

The stampede rattled the lines of thirty iron beds, fifteen each side of the ward, mostly filled with kids of various ages. The windows had been opened to dilute the disinfectant smell and a cross-breeze bulged the faded curtains that were drawn round beds to conceal the mysterious goings-on inside.

Mother looked down at me with a tear in her eye. She suffered for her children far more that we suffered from our own injuries.

'You'll be all right, Bobby,' she said. 'They're letting you home tomorrow with the plaster on,' as she handed me a bag of my favourite liquorice all-sorts. 'You will have to be careful though, and in six weeks you will be as good as new.'

Brother John could recognise sweets when he saw them and soon indicated, by sign and noise, what was required to keep him quiet.

Babies were ordered in those days; two years or less in-between seemed to be the accepted gap. In my father's case, he might have been trying to emulate his own mum and dad, my grandparents, who were from farming stock and had raised nine boys and three girls. If that was so, we still had a way to go.

Baby John was the third surviving Freeman, but one other had already died. The first-born, Freddie, named after my father, had died at ten months of pneumonia, a common cause of children's deaths in 1929. A picture of Freddie sitting on Mother's lap, with proud Father standing behind, used to hang in its egg-shaped frame over the mantelpiece. The picture disappeared as we grew older and curiously Mother wouldn't talk about it.

Maybe this tragedy made Mother worry more than most for her three surviving children. Great joy must have followed Victor's birth in November 1930, as he grew into a strapping, strong lad.

I followed on, slightly ahead of schedule, arriving in January 1932. Brother John and I were born at Assay Barracks, Tidworth but Vic was born in Redford Barracks, Edinburgh, hence the name

7

Victor Kier.

My birth came weeks after the regiment left Edinburgh, but the city must have held pleasurable memories for the young trooper, Frederick Freeman and his beautiful, slim wife Violet, for they christened me Robert Bruce.

Plastered up to my knee I left the hospital and was soon out playing again with the little army.

The barracks at York was a lively place once reveille had been sounded. The heart of the camp was the stables, with barrack rooms above for the unmarried or unaccompanied troopers. You could be married but not qualify by either rank or service for a married quarter. Both stables and barracks were ill-lit and badly ventilated, and during the winter the electric bulbs were kept on all day long.

The smell of the horses, hay and leather permeated everything and the barrack room and soldier were bathed in the mixture both day and night.

Married quarters were at the back of the south barrack block and were uncomfortable, damp and dismal. The barracks had been built in 1750.

We could see the soldiers from our flat, and the whole noise of the camp, busy with its daily tasks, continually surrounded us. The metal clip clop of horses' hooves on cobbled yards mingled with noisy, autocratic and often sarcastic orders of authority. Parade ground commands carried clear across York and headed for the coast.

The odd musician was often taking early practice before his mates arrived—maybe "sweating on a stripe" and out to impress the bandmaster.

Father was gone like a shot, soon after reveille; the Army was his life and controlled his total being.

He was a smart soldier, a corporal no less, and sweating on his third stripe. To get on you had to be more than a good soldier, perfectly turned out, never late, impeccable in both dress, speech and subservience. The Army came first, last and in the middle, nothing—but nothing—was more important than to keep a totally clean sheet in the regimental records and in the minds of your superiors. The family was important but keeping it running smoothly was Mother's job—not to get in the way of Father's military duties.

There were the lighter moments in camp life and each level in the hierarchy had its own independent social scene. There were the officers, who seemed to me, in my young years, to have something going on most evenings in the officers' mess. Kids were given ample freedom to roam the camp where little harm could befall them. To be trodden on by horses' hooves was not uncommon, but we got our ears clipped if we were caught in the stables. There were few other dangers in the camp, so we roamed, watched and contrived.

Many times we watched beautiful ladies arriving in lovely long dresses outside the officers' mess. They were the extras, or partners, who saved the subalterns from dancing with the frosty old Colonel's or Captain's wife all night, while their husbands drank whisky and talked about tomorrow's chukka. One had a duty to dance with the fusty old senior officers' wives once during the evening—'the done thing, you know.'

The sergeants' mess had its share of dances and social evenings as did the corporals' mess. I just loved to see my mother dressed for a mess dance; photographs show she was a tall lady at five feet nine inches, and very slim. She had a slightly long face with smiling, soft blue eyes, sensuous lips, a perfectly proportioned nose and long black hair. Dressed up in her red high-heeled shoes, layered taffeta black dress and with a red sash round the middle, she looked beautiful.

'Give us a twirl, Mum,' Vic would say and Mother would push back two chairs and the table to make room and twirl between the table and the black, three foot high fireguard. Our grins couldn't be measured with a twenty foot tape and Mother's eyes were dancing with lights of happiness.

My first of many dices with death occurred at Tidworth Barracks, Salisbury Plain, when I was only eighteen months old. Mother told us the story in later years.

Brother Victor decided to hold me under water in a horse trough. Maybe I was getting too much attention and the first-born didn't like it. Fortunately, a soldier in the stables saw what was happening and removed the by now blue baby and rushed me to my mother in the married quarters, luckily only some two hundred yards away. She revived me by holding me up by the legs and shaking me violently, then made me sick by putting her finger down my throat and finally opened the oven door on the big, black fire grate and placed me in front of the open oven on a blanket.

God must have had a purpose for me, I thought as Mother

9

recounted the story in my early years, and much later my guardian angel appeared again.

'We need you alive,' she said, and the Nigerian soldier—drunk on cola-nut and palm wine—took his finger off the trigger of the loaded sten gun and withdrew the muzzle from my belly-button—but that all comes later.

The two years were up and, as ordered, right on time, brother Ernie appeared in the August of 1936 and now we were four boys. John was moved from Mum's bedroom and joined me and Vic.

It was pitch black outside; the forty watt bulb, covered in fluff and dust, threw minimum light over the three-quarter iron bed.

'Get up, boys. I've got a lot to do this morning,' said Mother, gently shaking Vic's shoulder.

'Oh, Mum—in a minute—it's still dark,' whined Vic.

I looked up at Mum, nose just above the blanket edge and felt John moving at the bottom of the bed. His legs didn't reach far, but he was a fidgit arse and was head-to-tail with me and Vic, who slept at the head of the bed.

'Do as your mother said and do it now,' commanded Father.

Our feet were on the floor before Father's last words were spoken.

It was freezing cold in the unheated army flat and although it was six in the morning, it seemed as if we'd only just gone to bed.

'Get dressed quickly—the inventory man's coming at eight o'clock,' said Mum.

Packing cases surrounded us; light squares and oblongs appeared on the walls where pictures had hung for the last two years, the nails breathing a sigh of relief at no longer having to support the heavy, hard, oak frames.

'Victor—empty the pos and start folding the bedding.'

'Yes, Dad,' replied Vic pulling on his short trousers.

No-one ever argued with Father.

We were off to Hounslow—to prepare the Regiment for overseas service.

Heavy footsteps, banging, and voices in various states of agitation were all around us, as every other flat dweller pursued the same end.

The ground-floor flats were the first to have their inventories of army furniture checked out—same old procedure every time we arrived or left a quarter. Dining-table—one of; chairs upright—six of; cooker—one of (top gas ring faulty). Cutlery, crockery and so on—all checked off. Now they were in the bedrooms.

'Three piss-pots, Fred? Only two are on this list,' said the stores sergeant.

'Vi must have borrowed one from the Dowtys at number two, she's only got the baby,' said Fred.

'See she gets it back right away, will you—I'm in there next.'

Chamber pots came in various designs, always depending on rank; ours was the "standard white—with handle."

We had personal things, of course, but the main household furnishings were the Army's and stayed put. Mum and Dad had packed their personal treasures, ornaments, best china, pictures, and all important—baby paraphernalia—the day before. They were well versed in moving house.

We entrained for Hounslow and what was to be yet another home to get used to, just for a short period in our nomadic existence. Moving house became commonplace over the next ten years and had its effect on the lives of all army children.

Father was promoted in 1937 to sergeant and was chosen for the escort party at the Coronation of King George VI.

The inventory man called again in that October and we set off for India to uphold the Raj, to defend the North West Frontier and keep those Afghans at bay.

2

IT WAS A COLD, WET AND OVERCAST DAY; everything was grey and drab. Mother was holding Ernie, Dad had John in his arms while Vic and I stood beside them along the ship's rails. There seemed to be noise, bodies and confusion everywhere.

Troopers, with excited, smiling faces, jumped and jostled all around us, waving their hands at the mass of moving bodies far below on the quayside. The gangplanks had been taken away and the babble of noise heightened.

A soldier's peaked cap did a slow motion glide to the water below accompanied by cheers from the unfortunate trooper's mates.

The ropes were cleared from the bollards as the band on the quayside struck up a rousing farewell.

The crescendo of shouting was lost in the blare of the ship's siren and tearful women waved madly at the mêlée below. We waved too, but there was no-one down there from the Freeman clan—it just seemed the thing to do.

The HMT *Somersetshire* sailed away on that 14th October 1937 to the mystic, east; we had no idea what life had in store for us, but it was all very exciting.

The voyage was broken with calls at Malta, Port Said, Port Sudan and Aden. Bombay was reached on 6th November. Over three weeks cooped up on a troopship was a long time for small children.

For an ordinary trooper and his family the voyage out was anything but a romance. The officers took over three-quarters of the ship including lounges and cabins; the troopers and their families were packed into the troop decks in the ship's bowels.

We were huddled together, bedrolls touching bedrolls, thirty families thrown together in one long room with one communal toilet which was constantly in use and stank throughout the sleeping area.

Early in the journey the weather was so bad in the Bay of Biscay that our room became a torture chamber of heaving, sick bodies, screaming babies and moving flesh as the ship was tossed from side to side. How mother found strength to care for her four offspring amidst all this confusion with absolutely nowhere to turn to for help is still a mystery, but inner strength she found from somewhere and her children were blessed with this inheritance.

Once we reached the Mediterranean, the seas calmed, the sun shone and life took on a totally new complexion.

These were exciting times, playing bingo—known officially through all the services as housey-housey—as the ship sailed through beautiful sunshine. Bits of orange peel were put on called numbers and the cards were handed in after each house.

Most meals were served by soldiers and taken on deck, no restaurants or messrooms for all the families. Food was basic and eaten on your lap; standard times, standard food always. Four meals a day, the last being supper at eight in the evening with ship's biscuits, lumps of cheese, mustard pickle and cocoa.

As was the way in large families, the older children were left to their own devices and I wandered the main deck with Vic and the other kids. The ship was rolling from side to side and the deck chair that I was standing in started to slide. It came to an abrupt halt on hitting the steel work, which threw me from the chair and split my head open. I spent the rest of the journey in the ship's hospital, head half shaved and twenty-four stitches holding my scalp together.

The East began at Port Said where the bumboat men came alongside and tried to sell their wares. They were not allowed on board ship, so everyone looked over the side and attempted to bargain for fruits, sweets, cloth or trinkets.

The traders were adept at throwing a rope with a basket attached up the ship's side. You pulled it up, put your money in, lowered it down and then pulled up your chosen goods.

After convincing the trader to let him see the goods first, one trooper promptly scurried away and secreted his treasure.

Such an outcry ensued, backed by all the bumboats alongside, who refused to trade, that the Captain persuaded the Army CO to muster all troopdeck soldiers and allow the trader to come aboard to pick out the culprit.

The troopdeck was searched and the goods found in the toilets. Luckily for the culprit, he could not be identified, so all had to suffer. The bumboats were banned from visiting the ship and the Regiment suffered its first, albeit minor, indignity.

The ship sailed on through the Suez Canal and eventually berthed at Bombay. At transit camp, we made our first acquaintance with the "kite-hawk", commonly known by the troops as the "shite-hawk."

When the newly arrived soldiers from Blighty drew food from the cookhouse and tried to take it across the twenty yards to the dining room to eat, the shite hawks would swoop down and clear the food from the mess tin at one pass. You learnt quickly to wave your arms like mad or attempt to cover your food, if that was possible, as mess tins weren't designed with shite hawks in mind.

Shite hawks were from the kite and eagle family. Brown in colour, with up to a three foot wing span, they appeared out of a clear blue sky without warning. One could look up, see nothing and hear nothing. Take three paces in the open and "whoosh," the tray and cutlery were scattered on the ground and the meat was twenty yards away in the shite hawk's beak and disappearing rapidly. They plummeted out of the sky like dive-bombers and I only saw the wings flap after they had stolen their prize. The shite-hawk, the largest hawk in the hawk family, was common throughout India and lived by scavenging.

It was at transit camp that I encountered my first topee: a cork hat, encased in brown cloth with soft lining. This was to be my permanent headwear throughout my stay in India and many a good hiding from my father had to be endured in the first few weeks until the topee became regularly and permanently fitted to my head.

The family were also issued with bedrolls, a canvas holdall fitted with two heavy, leather straps. It had two internal flaps which held sheets and pillows together with a sort of thin mattress filled with kapok. This was the "bistra" or bedding roll, a standard issue to all cavalrymen and their families.

One day and night in transit camp and then we were on the move again.

The heat and acrid smells were oppressive as we were bundled through crowds of noisy brown faces to board a train, which was to be our home for the next three days. Everything was new, exciting and frightening. The sun blazed down out of a clear blue sky as we entered the allocated carriage—which was red hot inside; soon we were streaming with sweat. Dad's topee was jumping about on his head as he shouted at the Indian porters carrying our luggage. Troops were everywhere and the locals—who knew we were newly arrived by our flour-white skin—attempted to extract the maximum number of rupees and annas, whether they were beggars, who accosted you at every step, trinket sellers or the porters themselves.

The train was groaning with bodies as it attempted to leave the station. A snail's pace was all it could manage and we sedately crossed India from Bombay to Allahabad.

The journey was a nightmare for all concerned, relieved a little bit at first by the strange country we were passing through.

When the train pulled into a station we would all crowd to the windows on the platform side and marvel at the crowds of people and the variety of activity. Father would step down on to the platform and be immediately surrounded by scores of vendors. Mother would lean through the open carriage door and try and direct him to the nearest source of whatever it was that we wanted—fruit chiefly, or sometimes the char wallah—whilst all the time she was herself beseiged by more vendors and by the omnipresent beggars, who swarmed everywhere like flies.

Indian families would camp on the station days before their train was due, spread out their mats and cooking pots and settle down to live on that spot until their train came. Railway staff and travellers alike ignored them; it was as if they were not there; nobody seemed to mind.

Around them the platforms were alive with a shifting throng of people of all ages, shapes and sizes. And animals were everywhere: dogs, chickens in baskets, pigeons and goats tied to luggage.

Dotted across each concourse, like anchored rafts in fiercely tidal seas, Indian hot food stalls assailed the air with pungent, spicy, foreign smells. Whilst, competing for space, on mats on the hot cement, brass trinkets were offered for sale, together with brightly coloured wooden toys, strange live birds of brilliant plumage in bamboo cages and fruit, fans, magazines and cheap books.

With one deft blow of his curved, heavy knife, the coconut seller would open a coconut and hand it to you to drink the cool and refreshing milk. There was always something new to see and the fascinating spectacle held us spellbound until the train moved on.

15

And everywhere—on every visible foot of bare cement or railway track—there was a scarlet splash as if of blood—which we learned later matched up with the dark brown, almost black, teeth of many an Indian peasant. It was the mark of betel nut.

The landscape for the most part was flat. The earth a drab reddish brown. A few trees managed to survive somehow and a single cow would occasionally be seen ambling along with an Indian boy driving it; where they were going to was always a mystery for there never seemed to be a village in sight in any direction.

When we did chance upon a village, the sedate pace of the train gave us ample time to observe.

The side of the rail track was always occupied by "chikos," the Indian children, holding out their hands and chanting "baksheesh"—begging for food or for money. Pitiful beggars were there in profusion.

The mud and straw huts seemed to have been placed with no forethought or planning but the bright, colourful saris of the womenfolk livened up the scene.

Each village had its equivalent of the English village hall, the banyan tree, a large tree that cast great shadows and was sometimes just outside the village, sometimes in its centre. It was the meeting place, the court, the community centre, the place where all great decisions were taken.

We stopped fairly regularly to stretch our legs, stiff from sitting on hard, slatted seats, on which we also slept every night. We also stopped to take our meals prepared by army cooks on portable stoves set up by the side of the track. We looked out through slatted windows and saw the landscape in slices. Father and Mother's patience ran thin and we older ones had our ears clipped; our crying started others crying as the engine puffed hot cinders through the open slatted carriage window into the already hot carriages.

Mother wiped us all with the same cold flannel which spread the grime more evenly over us and we were all greatly relieved when the train finally pulled into Allahabad station three days later.

It was Mark Twain who described India as "the land all men desire to see." This was a sweeping statement but certainly India does hold a unique fascination which few other countries can match. The profusion of sights, sound and smells is quite hypnotic.

The bazaars in 1938 were fascinating and exciting and, to

16

someone of my tender years, held no fear. I loved the colour of the garments, the babble of sounds—human and animal—and the smells, accentuated by the blazingly hot sun, were almost indescribable.

Rows of tatty stalls stood in the open, displaying foodstuffs including raw meats, fruit and vegetables, while others sold household goods, earthenware, cloth, brass-work, candles, lamps and trivia. Flies covered the meat and most other things.

An old goat tethered to a stake bleated at a sacred cow as it wandered aimlessly around the stalls. The Hindus worshipped the cow, which had freedom to go where it pleased and crap where it liked.

The privilege was extended to the Indians themselves in that they squatted at the road-side to relieve themselves; bare-arsed for all to see; public toilets had not been heard of. Women were more discreet, squatting, but covering the act with their saris draped over their legs. The sights, the smells and the noise became a way of life and didn't cause a second thought or glance after the first few weeks. Each bazaar had its quota of beggars, some with horrific injuries often said to be self-inflicted so as to gain a living more easily.

Much has been written and many films have been made about life under the Raj. Many writers, often ex-civil servants, talk of princes and palaces, politics, intrigue and upper-crust life. They write of the caste system and the extraordinary number of servants required to run a household: a sweeper, a pony groom, ayahs, a cook, table stewards, gardeners, bearers for housework, a head bearer and, last but not least, an English governess.

One story I read recently about a privileged British family also in India took place in 1938. This particular family had a large house, set in its own beautiful grounds with their own guard at the wrought-iron entrance gates.

One morning the Memsahib saw a dead bird by the front verandah and instructed the head bearer to remove and bury it but the next day the bird was still there.

The annoyed Memsahib asked the head bearer, 'Why have you not removed this bird?'

'It is a lowly task and against my religion.' he replied. 'I have told the cook to remove it.'

The story continues over the next few days as the Memsahib follows the questioning through her large retinue of servants—head

17

bearer tells cook, then cook tells table servants, butler, nursery bearer, guard, ayah, two gardeners, groom and eventually the lowest of the low in the household hierarchy—the sweeper.

Even the sweeper could not touch the dead bird and the story ends with the Memsahib sending to the bazaar for a beggar to remove it at high cost.

This was the accepted way of life of the British Raj, the Indian Civil Service, the superior beings.

But five rupees offered early enough in the hierarchy of servants would break the caste system in any household.

And often did.

Many parts of India are very beautiful, with fields of yellow mustard, maize and sunflowers in the spring, flowering acacia trees that burst into clouds of pink and white blossoms, all set off by the misty purple of langerstroemia. The gardens continually blaze with the red and gold of the rusty simal trees, the ghulmohurs with their feathery plumes of scarlet, orange and flaming red, the oleanders and magenta bougainvilleas.

Where all this beauty is found, mostly around converging rivers, or in the hills, or Bengal, now Bangladesh, the garden of India, a host of colourful birds may be found too: parrots, sun birds, orioles, long-tailed pies and owls among many others.

As a contrast, in the rest of India there are vast areas of drab open plains and scrubland where a few trees and birds struggle to live.

It was such an area we crossed in our train, for the plains were the chosen home of the British cavalry regiments.

3

THE WAY OF LIFE OF A TROOPER'S FAMILY in India under the Raj was vastly different from that enjoyed by the families of those privileged Brits in the Indian Civil Service. We didn't have a dozen or more servants ranging from governess to sweeper.

Our bearer/cook was called Javelcon; he and his wife looked after the daily cleaning of our house, the cooking and the daily shopping. Two ayahs, Natia and Hannah looked after us four boys and that was it.

We first met our servants the day after arriving in Allahabad. A six hour ride in a lorry brought us to the military cantonment of Trimulgherry. Scruffy, dirty and smelly, Vic and I followed behind Mum and Dad as the receiving NCO led us to our bungalow. He had already talked to Father and they were on Christian name terms.

'This will be your place Fred, quite handy for the stables,' he said pointing, although we could already see and smell them just three hundred yards away. 'I've retained the servants that looked after the last family—they had four kids.'

Fred smiled for the first time in days as he surveyed the bungalow and servants.

'Got to go now, Fred—others to sort out—I'll be back later to check the inventory and tell you about life here,' and off he went, raising a dust cloud from the hard packed ground.

The servants spoke some pidgin English, as they had worked for a number of families and I took to their great big smiling faces immediately. Natia was going to look after Vic and me, Hannah the two young ones. At that time, John was three years old and Ernie one year.

After our first delicious meal of clear soup with toasted bread animals floated on it, followed by a roasted chicken each, the size

19

of a pigeon, with rice and vegetables, we rated Javelcon's cooking highly.

It was our ayah who suggested baths. What a performance as Natia tried to undress us. Father heard the noise and came into the room.

'Do as Natia tells you, or you will have me to deal with,' he stormed. We didn't argue.

The zinc hip bath was filled with tepid water from the kitchen some twenty yards across a compound outside the back of the bungalow. Two embarrassed boys were bathed for the first of many times by smiling Natia.

She was about twenty years old as far as one could tell. With her gold nose ring and many bangles on both her wrists and ankles, she acted as an alarm clock in the mornings as she came to wake us up. She was very gentle, sweet-natured and a totally devoted foster mother who we were to love dearly as time went by. She wore a colourful sari and blouse top and had beautiful, long, black, oily hair. Her hands were soft and her dusty dry toes poked through her sandals.

That night we slept under our mosquito nets for the first time. Vic and I had a bed each—what luxury. Four poles fitted to each corner of the bed supported the net which tucked in under the mattress. A brass fan hung from the centre of the bedroom ceiling and we soon became accustomed to its constant whirring noise, and were so tired that we soon fell fast asleep.

Exploring the bungalow and the new barracks was an exciting adventure for the next few days—when we could shake off the caring attentions of Natia.

Trimulgherry is on the Great Deccan plateau, in what was in 1938, the Indian state of Hyderabad, ruled by its native prince the Nizam. It is situated some eight miles from Secunderband. The Regiment lived in its cantonment, with barracks, bungalows for families, military hospital, clubs, sports ground, riding school, rifle range and, of course, stables. Permanent barrack buildings formed the main military base with a large drill square in the centre. Lines of stables skirted the main buildings to the south.

The school room was next to the stables and was fitted with wooden desks with inkwells. The desks seated two and were in rows of five across and four deep. At the front of the room, a foot high platform placed the teacher well above the pupils. A blackboard stretched the width of the room and windows to three sides were covered with wire mesh to keep out air-borne wildlife and snakes.

Outside the schoolroom and about three hundred yards away across flat, barren scrubland lay two rows of identical other ranks bungalows, cavernous barns built in 1874 for the King's Dragoon Guards.

A solitary tree fought for survival between the classroom and the married quarters with a shite hawk sentinel permanently perched on its topmost bough.

The officers' quarters and mess were as far away from the lower ranks' as possible, right across the other side of the barracks to the north.

The hard mud track that served as a main road passed twenty yards in front of the other ranks' quarters, and came to the crossroads in front of the main entrance to the barracks, where one road ran off to the nearby village Trimulgherry and a smaller road to the YMCA.

At the crossroads was also our main waterhole with a mud hut, where the family who worked the water-hole lived. The hole, or well, had a system of coconut shells on a conveyor belt which was continually in motion, bringing water from the bottom of the well and cascading it into a trough which then fed dirty containers. The power for keeping the water flowing was an unfortunate little donkey who was tied to a shaft connected to an ingenious set of wheels, belts and pulleys. The donkey walked in circles round the well, sometimes with a chiko on its back, who occasionally beat it if it slowed down.

A row of trees skirted the road to Trimulgherry a quarter of a mile away from our cantonment. The village could be clearly seen from our end house, its dominating feature the twelve foot high walls of a circular lost animal compound, a very important and prosperous business venture for the owner. Rows of mud huts with flat roofs could be seen forming the main street, with piles of cow pats outside each of them, which served as fuel for the fire on cold evenings.

At last I had a proper classroom with real desks and inkwells where the prefect mixed powder with water and filled the inkpots daily. I was now nearly six years old, shy and sometimes given to stuttering in company. I felt sure Mrs Marks, our teacher, didn't like me. She called me Robert and seemed to pick on me for no reason.

From the schoolroom window I could see beyond the stables across three hundred yards of scrub to my parents' married quarter, which had three large bedrooms, one very large living-room and a washroom. There were verandahs at the front and to the rear where we kept a "chatty" earthenware pot—full of ice-cold water, which always reminded me of the story of Ali Baba and his forty thieves. Also at the rear was a hard-packed yard bordered by two-foot-high mud and straw walls, which I could clear in best hurdling tradition when Father was after me.

The kitchen was an outhouse some twenty yards outside the yard. The bearer had to bring the meals from the outhouse kitchen to the bungalow and many times the shite hawks swooped down and stole the main course from right under his nose. He never learnt, and Father used to give him hell.

The bearer lived in a small shack attached to the kitchen and managed to maintain his family there as well. His wife assisted him without officially being entitled to pay, but the Sahib and Memsab looked after them.

Vic and I soon settled into our new way of life; there was so much to absorb. Natia sat cross-legged on the verandah trying to teach us a few basic Hindu words. We sat opposite her and were fascinated with her soft accented voice.

'Jeldi,' she would say, making her fingers run across the verandah floor. 'You say, "hurry," Natia say "jeldi".'

'Why should we say "jeldi" if you know it means hurry?' said the wise Vic.

Our concentration on learning was distracted by a lizard, scuttling across the open spaces of the ruby-coloured earth, in fear of being spotted by the ever-circling shite hawks, which climbed higher and higher until they were specks in the sky, but still maintained a perpetual watch on every movement below, ready to do their kamikaze dive on the dead or dying. And their keen-eyed vigil was matched by that of the brown fork-tailed hawks, smaller in size than the shite hawk, but scavengers also, whose shrill, musical cry became as familiar as the neighing of the horses in the stables.

The sentry hawk perched on the top branch of the seventy foot tree outside the camp entrance had a view which encompassed the whole camp and married quarters. He perched directly above the tonga wallahs' taxi rank, lined up at the side of the road by the entrance. These four seater carriages, where the driver sat back to back with the passenger, lay alongside the waterhole. He must, I thought, be the look-out and relays messages to his brother hawks for their next dive-bomb attack.

We grew up knowing only our own world of army life and never considered that children could ever live any other way. Sergeant Cotton, whom I detested because he was always grumpy and shouting at his servants, lived next door. He always looked miserable, never spoke to us children, only scowled. His only daughter Lucy sat at the same school desk as me; she was six years old, pretty but very quiet.

Our bungalows had a ten foot gap between them and a small tree struggled to survive in this gap. Sergeant Cotton kept a pet monkey tied to the tree, a sweet little creature with a lovely round face and soft pleading eyes. I did feel sorry for that poor little monkey and would feed him a peanut or banana at every opportunity. I named him Mickey. Many times I was caught feeding him by Sergeant Cotton who shouted me off, threatening to tell my father. Mrs Cotton didn't mind; she'd seen me feeding the monkey many times and said nothing, just smiled.

One day, returning from school at midday with Natia, I pinched a banana off the fruit dish and went out to feed my little friend. He wasn't there; his harness lay under the tree still attached to the rope. I was heartbroken. I'd lost my little friend.

Natia sat by my mosquito net as I lay on my bed. We weren't allowed out in the afternoons for it was too hot.

'Don't cry, little one,' she pleaded.

'But my friend is dead; why is he dead, Natia?' I asked.

'Him no dead, him free,' she smiled back.

'No, he's dead, he must be dead,' I cried.

'Dry your eyes little one, him free, him happy, you be happy too, eh?' she smiled.

The next day Vic and I were being escorted home from school by Natia, across the scrubland by the lonely tree, when we heard laughter and high pitched shrieks of excited voices coming from further down the line of bungalows.

We ran off together in the direction of the noise as Natia tried to grab us; she trundled on behind us in her flip-flop sandals.

A crowd of excited servants stood shielding their eyes with their hands as they looked up at the roof of the Chisholm house. Sergeant Cotton, braces over shirt, improperly dressed, wiped the sweat from his forehead with his big hand as he bawled out

23

commands to the heavens.

I looked up and there he was, my little friend Mickey. I saw that Vic was grinning too. A brown hand appeared on my shoulder.

'I say him free,' beamed Natia. 'Him free, no dead.'

Two servants were on the flat roof trying to follow the ever-changing commands coming from the white man below. Mickey just sat there, watching everything, with a relaxed but mischievous smile on his little face. He seemed to be enjoying the game and would let the servants creep nearer and nearer as he eyed them, head turning left, then right, until they were about to pounce. At the very last moment he was gone as the servants met in the space he'd vacated. This brought screeches of laughter and gesticulation from the happy band of servant onlookers who had not seen such a good show for months. Everyone was having great fun—except Sergeant Cotton. He looked as if he was going to have an apoplectic fit any minute. Shouting, swearing and sweating he took up a new command position and sent two more reluctant servants up the ladder on to the roof.

'You come now,' said Natia to Vic and me, tugging at our hands.

'No, no,' I said, fearing that my little friend would be caught.

The four servants spread out across the roof, grinning inanely, and crept towards my little pal. Excited advice and encouragement was proffered in Hindi by the excited onlookers, and not so excited advice in English by the frustrated Sergeant Cotton. I held my breath as they approached my furry friend.

When I thought he had left it too late, he made a quick dash between two of the servants, took off in a graceful leap and landed neatly on the flat roof next door. He then sat on his haunches and smiled at the trainee captors across the ten foot void.

Applause and laughter from the ground and roof level greeted this display of aerobatics; in utter disgust and defeat the sweaty, improperly dressed sergeant stumped off to his bungalow. Round one to Mickey.

For three days Sergeant Cotton and his band of reluctant conscripts attempted to trap, catch, coerce the playful Mickey back into captivity but to no avail, other than to heighten, still further, the blood pressure of a certain sergeant and the joyous delight of the under-privileged servants.

On the fourth day we were sitting indoors having lunch;

Mother was feeding baby Ernie as Hannah looked on. Vic, John and I were sitting at the table under the slow moving brass blades of the ceiling fan. Javelcon had just placed some fine cut sandwiches before each of us. Then it happened.

A high pitched scream rent the air. The pitiful, terrified noise filled the room. I was off my chair in a flash and rounded the verandah corner to see where the noise was coming from. The sight that greeted my eyes will never be forgotten.

Sergeant Cotton had my poor little helpless friend Mickey strapped in his harness. The rope was untied from the tree. The ugly enraged sergeant was swinging Mickey in his harness and viciously slamming him into the side of the bungalow wall. Mickey was terrified and screaming continually as the sergeant vented his evil temper.

I rushed straight at the big sergeant, kicking and pounding his legs and stomach as I screamed at him, but my efforts were like that of a sheep attacking an elephant. Mother and Natia were trying to pull me away. Mrs Cotton came out while my brothers and the servants watched. I was dragged indoors, still kicking and screaming.

That night Father took his leather belt off for the first time. I was in disgrace. Mother pleaded, 'Don't hurt him, Fred; he's only a baby,' but Father was deaf to pleas. Mother was shut out of the bedroom but pleaded through the door slats as Father leathered my backside.

'You'll show me up no more, son,' he said angrily as he left me in tears and pain. I never forgot that first leathering; it stayed with me for years.

Little has been written of the lower orders in the vast hierarchy that existed in British India. The British soldier's India was far removed from the life of the Indian Civil Service.

The Military in India found that caste applied as much to them as it did to the Indians.

While the army officer came near the bottom of the officially published "Order of Precedence," what chance was there for a cavalry trooper? Within the world of the military cantonment the officer was king. He did his daily social rounds, played polo or went pig-sticking while the other ranks tried to overcome boredom, their children mostly forgotten, to be seen and not heard.

I often witnessed my father, a married man with a large family, being called by his surname—Freeman—and dressed down in public in front of his wife and family by a young officer who was on his first posting. Father never answered back. He stood to attention and accepted public humiliation which was wholly unjustified. The total insensitivity and lack of human decency shown by many young officers offended me, even in my young years, and I was to remember these indignities in years to come. They left their mark.

Our school-teacher, the childless Mrs Marks, big, buxom and bespectacled, was the wife of a sergeant and was to be our only chance of learning during our time in India. She had black hair and small black eyes in her podgy round face. She favoured girls.

From nine to twelve o'clock each day she took a mixed class of some twenty-two youngsters. At twelve o'clock the ayahs took the kids home, gave them lunch and then put them under their mosquito nets for siesta, as it was deemed too hot to go out to play. Playing was for the evening. Later Mother would appear at bedtime, beautifully dressed for a party. She would see us to bed, mosquito net tucked in, ceiling fan whirring away.

At night, under our mosquito nets, which gave us a feeling of security, we let our imagination run free as we listened to the sounds of the Indian night. Jangling Indian music from the local bazaar wafted in through the slatted bedroom windows, interspersed with the neighing of horses and sounds of movement from the nearby stables and, more distantly, wild dogs calling each other on the open plains. A distant hyena laughed maniacally. Tongas clip-clopped past the bungalow, with the dressed-up memsahibs off to another function in the mess. These sounds were my lullaby.

No woman was allowed out at night without an escort and usually a trooper would be detailed to accompany Mother if she had to attend any function, and they always carried a lantern. Often Father was not available to escort Mum as he was usually the organiser of such functions. A jackal on its own would run for cover if it saw a human but in pack they were very dangerous. Regular weekly mounted parties of officers and N.C.O.s were sent out to shoot both wild dogs—the pariahs—and jackals to reduce the dangers round the camps.

The hustle and bustle of the village—which came to life at night—would drift across the four hundred yards of scrubland and

26

cloak me in a comfortable, enviable blanket. Oh, how I wished I could be there surrounded by the mysterious smells in the half light.

The memsahib's duties were not onerous; most women left everything to their servants. The bearer did the cooking, according to the instructions given by the memsahib each morning. The ayahs looked after the children with love and care and virtually became mothers to the younger ones. In the first year in India John and Ernie received more attention from Mother than the rest of us, but they were still in the hands of the ayah for most of the day.

Many other "wallahs" served the household as and when required. Clothes were made to order by the "derzi," who would sit on his little rug on the verandah with his ancient sewing machine. Give him a pair of trousers or a shirt to copy and there he would sit, with a variety of needles stuck in his turban, each needle with different coloured thread hanging from it, and he would work away until the garment was finished.

The sandal maker only required you to put your foot on a piece of paper. He would then carefully draw round it and the next day he would reappear, wreathed in smiles, with your new sandals. The "dudh" wallah delivered milk daily.

Not surprisingly, the cavalry was the most horse-orientated section of the British community in India. Most families had their favourite horses. Mother's horse was called Pluto and Dad's Dazzle. Both horses belonged to the army but my mother and father regarded them as their own. Dad trained them at every opportunity and Mum rode Pluto daily.

Polo was the sport, and every officer who wished to progress in his career needed first to progress at it. Matches regularly took place and, together with the other camp kids, I earned many annas staying well behind the goal posts and retrieving the ball.

I was growing up fast and found that my chiko friend was as good a friend as any white. His name was Anil—God of Fire —and I took to playing in the local village and bazaars with him and received many a leathering from Father for doing so.

Ali was the same height and stature as I was but his olive-brown face wore a perpetual smile. His friendly big brown eyes held a little hint of mischief which was in sympathy to my attitude of life at this time. A lovely head of jet black hair that glistened in the sun's rays gave promise of a handsome young man in a few years' time.

I never found out his true age as he changed it every time I asked him. At first I felt a little shy and embarrassed due to my clean smart clothes and new sandals, whereas he was scruffy and barefoot.

These differences were soon forgotten as the weeks went by.

Why choose a brown friend, you may ask, when there were plenty of white boys of my own age to choose from? Well, they were honest, open—not devious. They showed true feeling, genuine love and care, without looking for reward. The white boys seemed different in my experience. 'What's in it for me?' That was their attitude. Hot and cold. Friends when they wanted something you'd got, money, marbles, fag cards, but they would switch their allegiance, favours, friendships daily, change direction with the wind. They were good weather friends, whereas Anil was an all-weather friend, someone you could definitely rely on. The colour of his skin didn't matter, it's what's inside the skin that counts.

Anil introduced me to eating chapatties and drinking goat's milk. I even tried chewing betel nut, a regular habit of the Hindu but I couldn't spit the red juice as far as Anil. It wasn't long before I found myself in hospital with dysentery. Ten days of starvation was the treatment and I was carried from the hospital too weak to walk, and spent the next two weeks crawling around the living-room floor.

My home-coming was memorable in two respects: the great happiness it seemed to give Javelcon and Natia—my brothers took it in their stride, but the servants were overjoyed—and the food.

'I have special feast for Chota-Sahib,' declared the beaming Javelcon as Mother, Hannah, Javelcon's wife, and my brothers looked on.

I was carried to my seat at the table and special feast it was. My first food for ten days—I couldn't wait.

Javelcon placed in front of me a plate of clear, brown soup and a bowl of toasted animals all nice and brown. He had carefully cut from slices of bread, tigers, elephants complete with trunks, lions and other animals—all beautifully toasted. He floated some on the clear, brown soup and his eyes shone at me with a child's happiness.

As if this show of affection wasn't enough he then excelled himself with the main course.

The dinner plate was set down in front of me and all eyes looked for my reaction. It was a perfect round miniature fort with soldiers in the turrets and drawbridge. I was so excited I couldn't talk. The fort was made of mashed potato, the soldiers of toast, and the centre was filled with fine mincemeat. What a home-coming, what love. Could it be, I thought, that he sees me as different from the others? Running around the bazaar and the village with the chikos—or maybe he feels sorry for me because the Sahib uses his leather belt so much. Whatever, it was good to be back.

My father used to sleep on the verandah every night as did many of the men. One night I heard a commotion and, quickly nipping from under my mosquito net, witnessed the bearer hack the head off a cobra, which had been halfway up my father's bed leg. When I got to the verandah the deed had been done. The cobra's body was still writhing about the bed leg, its flat head stationary some six feet away. Javelcon stood there smiling with his trusty kukri in his hand. The bearer had often warned the Sahib about sleeping outside and now had proved his point. My white-faced father came off his bed and rewarded the servant in the only appreciative way—rupees.

In the morning the snake was chopped into pieces and burnt under the lone tree between the stable and the married quarters. This was necessary as the family of the dead snake would now come looking for it, so the servant's advice was followed. Two more cobras were killed and burnt during the following week.

Anil gave me a mynah bird having first clipped its wings to prevent it flying away. It was the best present I ever remember receiving. I took it everywhere and before long it rode on my shoulder but would not speak a word. Mrs Marks refused to have it in school so it spent its day in a box, perforated with holes.

Our schooling consisted of learning the "three Rs." One of my biggest fears at school was reading lessons because of my shyness and occasional stuttering. Mrs Marks knew of my problem but still called on me from time to time, much to the amusement and delight of the other children.

One day such a reading lesson was taking place when she said, 'Robert, read the next passage.'

The usual giggling in anticipation took place and when it

29

subsided, I took courage in both hands, stood up as was required and commenced to read.

As feared, I mumbled a few words and attempted to pronounce one I had never come across before. The class was in uproar and tears came to my eyes. Once again I felt humiliated. I looked up from my book to find not only my classmates laughing but also Mrs Marks. Immediately something exploded inside of me and that inner rebelliousness, which was to develop further throughout the rest of my life, took over.

I grabbed the full inkwell from its hole in the front of the desk and I threw it straight at Mrs Marks. It missed her and splattered against the blackboard, hurling the entire contents in all directions.

Then I panicked and ran from the room, dashed into the stables, climbed a ladder and found myself in a loft over the horses. I buried down in a corner behind old saddles and leather-work sobbing my heart out with fear, knowing full well what was coming.

How much time passed before I heard voices I have no idea but my fear heightened to sheer terror as soon as I heard my father's voice ordering the soldiers, who were obviously searching for me. It wasn't long before I was discovered and carried down the ladder by one of the soldiers. I was terrified.

My father dragged me across the open ground between the stables and bungalow in record time, my feet hardly touching the ground. On reaching the bungalow he threw me into the bedroom and stood in the doorway looking down at me, his eyes smouldering with anger as he slowly and deliberately unbuckled his wide leather belt and pulled it from round his waist.

Natia was shrieking in Hindi as tears flooded her face. Javelcon was tugging her away towards the back of the bungalow. Mother was trying to hold Father's arm but he kept shrugging her off. 'Please, Fred, please—wait until you've calmed down—he's only ...'

'Stay out of this, Vi.'

'But Fred, you'll kill him, please Fred ...'

Father pushed Mother out of the bedroom and slammed the door.

'This will be the last time he shows me up in front of the regiment, now stay out Vi.'

The terror for me was in the waiting, trembling with fear as he removed that thick leather belt and then the blows rained down. I could always hear my mother crying out on the other side of the bedroom door but her pleas were to no avail. Father had been disgraced in front of his soldiers, and the Regiment. It would be the talking point of the garrison. That uncontrollable son of Fred Freeman.

Mother was told to keep me in the bedroom without food for two days.

'That will teach him,' said Fred and so one more good hiding was chalked up.

Mother would of course find safe periods to bring food to me, but she warned, 'Don't dare tell your father.'

So my formative years continued, and I learnt very easily the need to be crafty and at times devious in order to avoid a good thrashing.

4

A CANTONMENT IN INDIA was its own world. Your very existence was governed by its rules and practically no external influences were allowed to affect your way of life. The camp was your world and your world was the camp. Anything that happened was the news of the day and travelled faster than a brush fire. This was an insular world where everybody knew about everybody. *'Fred Freeman's unruly boy is in trouble again,'* and Father had to face his men and superior officers. What a disgrace.

N.C.O.s were godfathers to other N.C.O.s' children, their wives, godmothers; wives tended to acquire the rank of their husbands.

The colonel's wife was the female colonel and commanded all wives. A wife mustn't let her husband down by outrageous remarks, strong opinions or by disagreeing with the wife of someone of higher rank. You knew your place.

The poor cavalry trooper was the biggest sufferer of all. Often banned from the nearest town and local village, his life was the cantonment and boredom. This boredom was softened to some degree by the number of wallahs that removed from him some of the onerous tasks of soldiering that would have been his lot in Blighty.

The nappy wallah would shave him while he was in bed and the char wallah would bring him a cup of tea. His uniform would be pressed, courtesy of the chokas. This could be expensive, but most soldiers were good bargainers and enjoyed treats. Other official wallahs fried eggs in a large pan, the dudh wallah brought milk and pats of butter, the ham wallah was a fellow with a great roll of ham on a board and cut slices for one anna each. There was the ever present sweet wallah, the dhobi wallah, who returned the clean laundry and even the corn-cutting wallah who did great business with his horn-shaped tube and, with patience, would draw out a corn with its roots.

The result of all these wallahs was a slightly higher morale. No longer did the trooper have to muck out the stables first thing every morning; that was now done for him. The soldier, who had tasted this small amount of power usually reserved for the rich, was now less hassled and quite a bit smarter in appearance.

Many of the menial tasks were carried out by Indians according to caste. The Regimental water carrying—a most important task—was done by bheestis—very low in caste terms.

Even lower came the mehtar, an ironical name—literally meaning prince—for someone who performed a vital job. Latrines were holes in a board behind corrugated sheets. It was said that one could be sitting there, thinking great thoughts, when a brown arm would snake out and remove the tin tray below your backside. This was the dedicated mehtar at work, filling his "Bombay milk-cart," bullock-drawn, and taking its contents for burial.

It seemed everybody had their place in the grand order of things.

'Don't go near that smelly bazaar,' Mother would say.

She was right; it had one smell and many smells. The men there were always urinating and crapping, so you kept clear of certain obvious places. Spitting, too, as they cleaned their teeth with neemstick—a soft woodstick—under the communal tap, or blew their noses between their fingers.

The smell of hot cow-pat fires, spiced curries cooking, chapatties on griddles. Cow and goat crap everywhere. The smell of fresh fruit, perfumes, sweaty bodies oozing garlic odours in a five foot circle of the owner. Meat and vegetables offered free meals to a million happy fat flies, which, although overfed, preferred the cows' sores, crap-covered backsides, or babies' gummed eyes.

Yes, there were many smells in a bazaar and together with the colourful saris and turbans, and the bustle of human flesh, it was a fascinating and exciting place to be, so, with Mother's warning in my ears, I sloped off to find my friend Anil.

Anil's house was on the outside of the village and was

33

separated from the main clump of housing. They were one of the poorest families as their house bore witness. It was just fifteen feet long and six feet wide, and so low that Anil's father couldn't stand upright in it.

It was built of mud and straw, but the roof—as Anil proudly pointed out—was covered with badly flattened, old kerosene tins. A three foot doorway with no door gave entry through one of the long walls. A scraggy, skeletonised cow and two goats, their greatest possessions, took up one third of the floor area which was covered in straw. Anil and his two younger brothers lived with their parents in the other two thirds, separated only by a low mud wall. A fire hole cut in the floor for cooking indoors in inclement weather completed the design.

They were a young family. Anil's mother had married at the age of eleven years and was now seventeen. It was customary to marry very young as puberty came much earlier in the eastern climate. Anil's parents were casual traders in the bazaar, selling fruit and vegetables from tin trays. They didn't own a stall or pitch of their own and their youth was against them in their culture. Anil's father was hoping to get work at the army cantonment when he grew older.

I visited them as often as I could, but Natia was getting very upset at my absences. I was treated like a lord by Anil's mother, who always wanted to cook a chapatti or give me a drink of goat's milk.

I became quite good at using my toes; Anil could fire a stone from under his big toe and hit a can ten feet away, or more. With my sandals stuck down my trouser waistband I would compete with him and other chikos. No contest really, but I became fairly proficient and got a lot of excited laughs and jumping about when I did hit the target, and a bit of strap from Father on the occasions he found out about it.

In the evenings the bazaar took on a further dimension of life with people, noise and smells. Smoke and flames from the fires helped light the way down the narrow bazaar and village paths.

The hath-batti brass lamps lit the better-off shops and stalls, whilst the traditional "five anna" earthenware pot showered light from a wick floating in oil in the classical lamp of the poorer establishments. Music entered the bazaar arena as old gramophones blared out scratchy Indian tunes from open doorways. The professional letter-writer, with round wire spectacles perched on the end of his nose, sat cross-legged on his mat, behind his folding desk, continuing his business in the light of his hath-batti, earnest client gesticulating in front of him.

My spirit of adventure could not be quelled by illness or beating, and at every opportunity I would slip away to the village to see my friends.

One night, lying under my mosquito net, I heard the sound of drums coming from the direction of the bazaar and crept from my bed to investigate. I was too young to realize the dangers of going out in the dark, not least of which were hyenas roaming in packs.

It was a clear, chilly night as I made my way across the open scrubland and the drums drew me on. I crept round the back of the mud huts fronting the bazaar and saw in the moonlight crowds of people around a pyramid of dried saplings. Perched on top, and tied into an old colonial chair, was a familiar face, the dead face of the village elder.

As I stood there, the drum stopped and the flames started—the wailing started too. I witnessed my first Hindu pyre.

My friend, the village elder, councillor and wise man, was going to meet his Maker in the best tradition of the Hindu faith. I crept back to my bed in tears and no sleep came that night.

In my many visits to the bazaar in the first year at Trimulgherry, the village elder—the wise one—had always smiled kindly on me. He spoke good English and I am sure he knew I had an affinity with the Indian race. Even the young whites were taught that they were superior to the Indians and they often aped their seniors in their day to day contact with them. For some reason I was different. Don't ask me why, I never did know. But the village elder did.

As kids who were left to their own devices, like all kids, we found ways to amuse ourselves. The mode of transport for the whites was the tonga wallah or ticca garry. This was a horse or pony drawing a large two-wheeled cart, much like the pony and trap. But it had a roof to guard against the hot sun, and a bench-type seat on which the driver sat back to back with his passengers. The tonga wallah's taxi rank was just outside the barracks and, awaiting a fare, once he got in the queue, the driver would alight and climb in the back seat, sprawl out and fall asleep. My gang took great delight in belting the horse and seeing the tonga disappear in a cloud of dust, the driver trapped where he lay.

The sweet wallah didn't fare any better. He carried a large trunk on his head. I would show my money and the trunk was opened. Its top had a lift-out section which was divided into small compartments, containing samples, sweets cut into two or three pieces. The customer could try a sample before buying and I became adept at stringing the seller along and often tasted half his wares before deciding not to buy.

'Ah, the chota sahib is one clever sahib, I think,' said the amiable vendor.

As for the camp cinema, Father would give Vic and me the three annas entrance fee, but it didn't cost us anything to get in as, after paying the first time, we loosened two boards in the back row and thereafter entered from under the cinema once the lights had gone down. I would buy a paper cone of peanuts at the interval for one anna and had two annas to add to my secret hoard.

It was the rainy season and I was sitting at my desk in the classroom dreaming of my mynah bird as Mrs Marks rambled on. My hand had been raised for some time but teacher ignored it. I stood up with my hand still raised.

'What is it, Robert?'

'Please can I go to the toilet, miss?'

'Yes,' she said.

As I moved forward, her voice cracked like a rifle.

'Where do you think you're going? Sit down.'

Nonplussed and with the other children giggling, I could feel my face burning red; I sat down but I was bursting to pee. I tried it again and received the same treatment.

My partner at the double desk was Lucy Cotton and without a second thought I proceeded to pee on her gumboot, I suppose, in desperation, thinking she wouldn't dare tell. She let out a yell as she moved away and I was left peeing on the floor.

Of course Father was sent for; nobody asked the question of me, 'Why?' but after another severe thrashing and starvation, Mrs Marks did say to me on my return to class, 'You CAN do anything, but to get my permission you must say, MAY I?'

A bit late to tell me now. Grown-ups are funny people, I thought looking up at Mrs Marks as she explained it to me. Parents, ayahs, and teachers, they never ask me anything, they always know what's best for me. They never ask me *why* I do this or *why* I did that; if they don't like what I've done, then they just belt me. Why do they always know what's right; what's good for us?

Despite the strict upbringing, I still had a great respect for my father. Fred was a magnificent sight in his blues. Six foot one inch, straight up, very slim and agile. Sharp pointed features to his narrow face, bright, mischievous, blue eyes, and a born winner in any competitive arena.

Gymkhanas were a regular feature of army life. They offered an opportunity of showing off one's riding skills to the rest of the Regiment and local dignitaries. There were races and competitions for all soldiers and their wives; many of the ladies were good horsewomen.

Marquees were set up for refreshments; the competition area was roped off with coloured bunting and the band played gentle music all afternoon as competition followed competition in the arena.

A sight that stirred my blood and made me very proud of my Dad was the gymkhana's finale, tent-pegging.

A tent peg was placed in the ground, and one by one the competitors attempted to remove it at full gallop on the end of their lance.

We danced around Mum with excitement as we waited for Dad's turn—then his name was announced over the tannoy system.

Fred, in full uniform, lance tip pointing to the sky with pennant flag fluttering, and base of lance fitted into his right boot lug, sat erect on his beautiful, black stallion some forty yards away, waiting for the starter.

I stood with Mother, brothers Vic, John and Ernie, all in line with the tent peg and behind the roped-off area. The whole regiment had turned out for this sporting day and the arena was packed all round.

The starter dropped his flag and Fred started his run. His lance came parallel to the ground and tucked under his right arm within the first fifteen yards. Then, as his horse thundered on and the spectators gasped, his body started to lean to the right; lower and lower he leaned as the horse galloped faster and faster. The arena went quiet and only the thunder of the horse's hooves filled the air. All eyes were on my Dad. His body was almost parallel with the ground, his lance was perfectly still and his eyes were fixed on the peg, ten feet ahead. He came by in a "whoosh" of speed, the tip of his lance entering the centre of the wooden peg. In a flash he was upright on his horse, standing in his stirrups, and as the horse galloped on he let out a terrifying but triumphant yell, holding his lance and tent peg high in the heavens for all the Gods to see. Rapturous applause broke in a wave all round the ground. I beamed up at Mum with pleasure and pride, and noticed a teardrop on her smiling face. At times like this I was so proud of my Dad.

The two years were up; Mother became pregnant again in 1938 and went into confinement in Trimulgherry Hospital in September.

We were eagerly awaiting her return and the ayahs bathed and dressed Vic, John, Ernie and me in preparation for her home-coming.

As she entered the door carrying a bundle of shawls she bent down to show us our first sister. We were so excited. My first look at baby Pauline was one of amazement.

'Why isn't she brown?' I asked. Mother repeated that story many times.

5

A NEW BABY in the Freeman household was always the signal that the army was about to announce a move, and, within a fortnight of Pauline's birth, the Regiment entrained for Risalpur in the north. Risalpur, literally translated, means "full of cavalry" and was the main military base controlling the defence of the North West Frontier.

The train journey from Allahabad took three days to complete and passed through many towns including Agra, Cawnpore, Delhi, Lahore, Rawalpindi and Peshawar.

When the cavalry were on the move, the soldiers served the meals from mop buckets. We all had a tin plate, knife and fork. A soldier carrying a bucket of fried bacon waltzed down the train and was followed by others with beans, fried bread, ordinary bread and bully biscuits. These were dumped on your plate and my stomach became accustomed to the basics of life. My favourite was the char wallah; I loved my tea.

Sometimes it took up to a week to move from one cantonment to another by lorry and train, and we were privileged to taste the real life and culture of the Indian people. Today, however, this is lost on the traveller as distances are wiped out by aeroplane, modern transport and the international opulence of five star hotels

The army was, for once, considerate in allowing troops three hours to visit Agra. That unforgetable first sight of the Taj Mahal has remained with me vividly: one of the most memorable experiences of our stay in India. Little did I realise at the time, that the Taj Mahal was, and still is, one of the great wonders of the world and certainly one of the most beautiful.

Twenty thousand men and women laboured for twenty-two years, from 1631 to 1653, to complete it, a labour of love unequalled in history. This amazing mausoleum was built by the Shah Jahan as a glorious monument to his wife, his only love,

Mumtaz-i-Mahal.

The Taj Mahal is beautiful not only because of its perfect shape and its translucent white marble, but also because of the matchless skill of the craftsmen who created the delicate interior marble screens which made it the most outstanding structure in India.

I well remember arriving at the railway station where, as well as the usual assortment of traders and beggars, there were dozens of brass wallahs seated in rows tapping away with little toffee hammers on twelve inch round brass plates to create perfect engravings of the Taj Mahal which they then filled with various coloured ochres. They also made cigarette boxes, egg cups and perfect tongas with ponies. Mother bought many fine examples which have pride of place in the Freemans' homes today.

When we got back on the troop train Father told us his version of the building of the Taj Mahal. According to him, the Shah Jahan was so distraught at losing his beautiful wife he employed hundreds of workers to build it over many years. A secret compartment was created in the marble tomb for his wife's ashes, and in order to ensure that the secret location was never betrayed, all of the workers were either killed or had their tongues cut out. I was so sad listening to this story that it has always remained with me.

The year spent in Risalpur followed the same pattern of army cantonments but the troopers were now on active service. Week long patrols were sent out along the frontier.

The mountain tribes, especially the Pathan warriors, made regular raids into the villages of the plains and carried off women, cattle and, when they could find them, guns and ammunition. Three hundred Indian casualties had been sustained in the previous year. Nevertheless, regiments vied with each other to serve on the North-West Frontier. It was one of the few places where active service was to be found. It was both honourable and exciting.

The temperatures rose to one hundred and twenty degrees Fahrenheit in the dry season and the heat was too much for the families, so in March or April each year the annual migration "up the Khuds" to the hill stations took place for mothers and children.

On a cold and misty March morning, the convoy rolled; wives and children hanging over the sides of lorries, waving madly to fathers and husbands, their excited faces peering through the clouds of dust sent up by the turning wheels.

To reach the nearest hill station could mean a journey of two days or more, which was undertaken in three ton canvas-covered trucks with Indian army drivers. Clothing and some family possessions had been loaded under the watchful eyes of the wives, and the lorries were packed until they were half full. The canvas tops were neatly rolled forward and tied in position. The rest of each truck was for women and children: the wives of course taking the wooden seating by the tailboards and the children supposedly safely positioned between mothers and furniture. Three or more families per truck left little room for manoeuvre.

While most husbands were required to "soldier on," continuing their duty of patrolling the North West Frontier of India, a few lucky men were detailed to accompany, and guard, the families during their stay in the hills.

This was an exciting time for the children and I retain many a memory of both the journey and the months spent in hill stations. The government had its own well laid-out and established hill stations: Mussourie, Simla, Naini Tal and Darjeeling.

Of the eighty hill stations developed by the British as retreats from the heat and hazards of the plains Darjeeling was probably the best known. Built seven thousand feet up in the Himalayan foothills and looking across Kangchenjunga, it was to this retreat that the Bengal Government moved in the hot season. It was a small town with its own solidly built church, Government House, Anglican school, post-office, bandstand, public gardens, shops, library, and permanent residences of two or three storeys high, which would not have looked out of place on the banks of the Thames at Henley. It was an escapist's paradise, where women outnumbered men, and a full social programme made for a life of leisure for those of high rank and the well-to-do.

Simla, north of Delhi, equally well laid out, was home to the Viceroy in the hot season. From this place he ruled in absolute power over several hundred million people. The Viceregal Summer Palace dominated the town and the hills were covered with a flock of white bungalows. Simla's Mall, the main thoroughfare, was lined with reputable jewellers, tailors, booksellers, hairdressers, clubs and hotels. The town had a cricket pitch, polo fields and even boasted a racecourse. For at least a third of every year it was one of the great capitals of the world.

Needless to say, such grandeur was not for the likes of the lowly cavalry regiments' families. The small, remote hill station to which they were assigned was called Ghorra Daka, but the troops' name for it was the much more descriptive "Hell's Kitchen." It was set between two great hills and accessible only by means of a rough dirt track road. With only two stops we travelled all day and reached the base of the foothills by early evening. The soldiers pitched a few tents, while servants sought wood and cow pats and lit the fires. Stripped naked and washed down in cold water by the ayah, and then freshly clothed, we tucked into supper. The soldiers carried round buckets of half-mashed potato and of savoury minced meat, smacking as much as you wanted on to your tin plate. Another soldier's buckets contained chunks of bread and thick lumpy gravy. We cleaned our plates without any trouble.

Bedrolls were laid out on top of groundsheets and sleep came quickly. Little did we know what was in store for us on the morrow, which was just a well.

As the sun rose through the chill morning mist, the camp was astir. Variety was not the spice of life in the cavalry cook book, and the predictable bucketfuls of bacon and beans were devoured, along with strong sergeant major's tea, so called because of the generous addition of condensed milk to thicken the brew.

The Indian drivers slopped petrol out of cans into the fuel tanks of the lorries and it was "All Aboard!" and off we went, heading for the Khyber Pass.

The mountains rose steeply in front of us and the stony road was hewn out of the side of the mountain, its width more suitable to bullock carts than to three-ton trucks. The road wound on through rocky gorges. Herds of goats grazed like little toy animals far below, where a shiny silver ribbon of river ran through a green tree-lined valley.

The drivers were notorious for going as fast as they could and as we ascended, with trucks almost touching the mountain on one side and a sheer drop on the other, nervous voices were raised.

In the narrowest section of the road and at sharp bends large boulders had been placed on the edge of the precipice, presumably to keep vehicles clear. The drivers were oblivious to danger, or so it seemed, and drove at such a speed that we were all made to sit on the floor of the lorry and the grown-ups' fear was rapidly transmitted to the children. The nightmare continued for some hours. On rounding yet another bend, our truck came to a screeching halt and we were thrown everywhere. Scrambling upright, we were terrified to see that we were literally teetering on a precipice. And half a mile down in the gorge below was the crumpled mess of the lead truck which had just gone over.

It was one of the cooks' trucks and no whites were on board. A party were detailed to stay behind to do what they could, and the rest of the convoy set off again, this time at a more careful pace, with the most trusted driver in the lead, accompanied by the sergeant in charge.

We made the Khyber Pass by mid-afternoon and were disappointed to find that the famed border between India and Afghanistan was basically a chain across the road, with two armed Indian guards and a small sentry box. Beyond was an open space dynamited out of the mountain, and military huts where the guards lived. I was fascinated by the little monkeys that came scrounging on to our lorry and would actually eat bananas held up for them.

We arrived at Hell's Kitchen shortly after leaving the Kyhber Pass to find it only consisted of bungalows, no open areas, no community buildings, nothing in fact but living quarters. The bungalows were set on three levels up the mountainside interconnected by wide tracks. Tall fir trees covered the slopes below, falling away steeply to a mist layer at the bottom of the valley. All the bungalows were square identical timber boxes fronted with a verandah covered in fly mesh, and each comprised a large living-room, two bedrooms and a kitchen. The back door opened on to a small clear area of rocky ground and the fir forest continued up the mountain. One of these was to be our home for the next six months.

Two memories stand out of incidents during our stay, the first of which would be regarded as almost unbelievable if it happened today. It would read more like fiction.

Within the first month, an eighteen month old baby went missing. The mother was inconsolable and several search parties were arranged. Soldiers and Indians alike scoured the camp, the local village and bazaar, all to no avail. That night all families were locked in their bungalows, extra guards were posted and the whole camp slept in fear.

The next day, an Indian tracker reported signs of baboons entering the camp. An armed search party set off into the fir forests below. Later that day it returned with a tale to tell and the eighteen month old baby was returned—unharmed—to its unbelieving mother.

43

The story was told that a family of baboons had kidnapped the baby and were found treating it as their own. Unfortunately the whole baboon family had to be shot to rescue the child, and from that day on, small children were never left unattended.

Halfway through our stay up the Khuds, Father came up for a spot of leave. He'd been with us about a week when the second incident occurred.

Ernie and Pauline slept in Mum's room. Vic, John and I shared a bedroom. Our double bed was positioned under the one window. During the night a loose wallah had removed a pane of glass above our bed, unfastened the window, somehow passed over us sleeping boys and entered the bungalow.

Loose wallahs were the canniest, most cunning burglars ever encountered. They operated completely naked, except for a belt around their waist sporting a dagger. Their body was entirely covered with cheetah fat which was claimed to have two advantages—firstly, it repelled dogs by its smell and secondly, it offered no grip whatsoever to anyone trying to catch them—hence the name "loose" wallah.

This particular fellow must have been very practised in the art of thieving. It was later deduced that he wrapped every item to stop them from rattling, and placed them in a large tablecloth before making his escape without disturbing any of the sleepers. It was only next morning that the burglary was discovered.

Father immediately formed a posse with the Indian Military Police and commenced searching the local village. Vic and I followed with our gang at a distance to watch the proceedings.

It was a tremendous surprise to me when Father spotted his possessions without any difficulty, openly displayed in the village bazaar. Whether the stall holder was the actual thief, a relative of the thief, or just a middleman will never be known, but, he paid the penalty which I witnessed with some horror.

He was dragged screaming his innocence through the bazaar, tied to a post and, his shrill screams echoing throughout the hills, he was flogged unmercifully by one of the Indian policemen. The large crowd of villagers that witnessed the flogging made no protest but, crying inconsolably, I ran home to Mother and suffered many a nightmare over this ugly scene.

We came down from the hills in late August and returned to permanent barracks and my friends in the bazaar.

6

WHEN BRITAIN DECLARED WAR ON GERMANY in September 1939, it was generally expected that the Regiment would be ordered home. But that order came much more swiftly than we thought. We were to depart in December—barely three months after the declaration. Preparations for departure got under way immediately and the box wallah was in great demand. Father had large, square, wooden trunks made, each painted black with his name, rank and regiment stencilled on the outside. I was to see these trunks packed and unpacked many times in the years to come as we moved from place to place.

We embarked on a special troop train for the journey from Risalpur to Bombay and for three days we saw India in the raw as we passed through town and country.

The saddest story told by my parents in later years was of how all the horses were shot. Apparently, orders from on high forbade the Regiment to leave its horses in the hands of the Indians, and some poor devils would have had the terrible duty of killing their utterly trusting animals. The children, thank God, were unaware of this at the time. Instead, they suffered the heartbreak of saying goodbye to the servants.

The servants were more, much more, than gophers or skivvies. They had been with the family—had, in fact, been *a part of* the family—for nearly three years and had travelled everywhere with us. Their future was now totally uncertain. They cried bitterly along with the children. As the train pulled out of Risalpur station, we watched them until they were specks in the distance, and it was a horrendous heartbreak for us all. We lost our ayahs. We lost second mothers who, for many, had been more dearly loved than the first.

We arrived in Bombay in the middle of the night, dirty and smelly; Father's patience was thin, so we kept close to Mother.

Somehow Father manoeuvred his family tribe, with considerable luggage and much bawling and shouting at Indian porters, to a warehouse where the families camped and slept until morning. Everything was done military style and Father's place in the pecking order saw us, as a sergeant's family, called for boarding at midday.

My first impression of the seconded P & O ship H.M.T. *Ettrick* was her enormous size. For all that, once the Regiment was on board there wasn't room to spit. Mothers and children were allocated troopdeck cabins and longrooms. All troopers had to sleep on deck. Dad was lucky; he bagged a place next to the funnels.

'It'll keep me warm when we get past the Med,' he said.

We set sail on 14th December 1939 as the sun was sinking and I could not sleep for the excitement of it all.

The first leg of the voyage was fairly uneventful. Christmas Day 1939 was celebrated by all ranks at Port Said, where parties were held on board. On Boxing Day we embarked on the final leg of the voyage home, but first all families were mustered on deck and received a talk from the C.O. and Captain.

We were told there was a war on, as if we didn't know, and the *Ettrick* was part of a convoy. German submarines were a threat and although we had the protection of the Royal Navy, we were nevertheless to follow strict procedures. We were obliged to wear our life jackets day and night, even to sleep in, and if anything was ever designed NOT to sleep in, it was these so-called life-jackets. Secondly, when the alarm sounded, we were to make our way—without panic—quickly to our allotted lifeboat, which we were to stand alongside.

The C.O. then explained that lifeboats would only be allocated to wives, other females and children under sixteen years. The ship was so full there was no room in the lifeboats for men. Also the men would not attend boat drill with the families, as their muster point was elsewhere. After this cruel lecture, many wives broke down and cried and the children joined in.

As we left Port Said, the final farewell ritual was played out, and a sign was sent to me from above. I didn't recognise the sign at the time but I have often thought of it since.

As the ship sailed into open waters, everyone was paraded on deck with their topees, which at a given signal they all flung overboard. Then they cheered and everyone was smiling and chattering away. Father looked down at me, still clutching my small battered topee.

'Throw it, son,' he said. I looked up at him.

I didn't want to throw it; I liked my topee, for it was my friend and had been everywhere with me. I hadn't liked the hat in the beginning and I'd taken a few wallops before I accepted it. Now I would probably get walloped if I didn't get rid of it. Grown-ups were funny people; they didn't seem to understand us at all. With sad heart I let my topee fall. There it bobbed, on its own, quite a distance from all of the others disappearing astern.

That was the sign. I would always be a loner, outside the crowd, never in step, doing my own thing.

As my topee fought the waves, I felt a pang of sadness trying my hardest to keep it in sight until eventually it was lost on the vast endless sea.

Farewell India, and thank you for a memorable beginning to life.

The H.M.T *Ettrick* sailed on into its uncertain future.

The Mediterranean sunshine made the days pleasant, and ship's games were arranged to soak up the time and energy of both children and adults. Various deck sports were arranged by the crew and children's competitions kept us occupied for much of the time.

'Look after your brothers and see they don't get into trouble,' said Father to Vic, leaving us after lunch with the assembled kids, for another games afternoon, this time organised by three troopers.

'Yes, Dad,' said Vic, as John and I stood there.

'And don't go wandering off again,' Father said, looking straight at me.

'No, Dad.' And off he went.

Vic was separated out with other big lads to play football. A pitch had been chalked out on deck and a rag football had been fashioned by the troops. Deck chairs were goal posts and there were at least fifteen players on each side.

John and I were taken further along the deck where army hoopla apparatus was positioned. Broomsticks in upright lines and thick rope rings were the hoops. I didn't want to play this daft game and said so.

'I want to play football with my brother.'

47

'You do as you're told, son; there's too many footballers now,' said the soldier.

I hated anybody telling me to do as I was told; this always brought out the worst in me.

'Stand in line, son, and wait your turn.'

Bugger you, I thought. You're not me Dad, so when he wasn't looking I sloped off back to the footballers.

Vic was a large lad for his age, big boned and broad with it; he was to turn out to be a real muscle man, and already he had a wicked sense of humour. He love winding Mother up at every opportunity, doing things he knew would attract her attention. His favourite was cramming his mouth full to overflowing as soon as food was put in front of him. Then he would look at her, cheeks bulging, with a huge smile on his face, and the devil in his eyes waiting for her reaction. Mum couldn't tell him off without laughing and that was exactly what Vic wanted.

Now here he was, charging around like a bull in a herd of heifers, knocking both opponents and team mates over in his sheer enthusiasm for living. His team was winning according to the blackboard. Ponies 1, Nags, 5, Vic being a Nag. The ball came out of a clutch of players into a clear area of deck and the bull charged. He took a mighty kick and the ball rose to new heights across the pitch, over the rails and was never seen again. Vic's team won as there was no spare ball, and I swear to this day it was a deliberate act, but the innocent face presented to the organiser would have convinced an angel that it was an accident. Innocence was Vic's speciality. Dad's was something else.

Evening concerts were occasionally organised on the troopdeck and for the first time I saw my father in a different light. He loved the stage and being in the spotlight in front of an audience, and he was good. Recitations were his forte with occasional songs about "The old grey mare she ain't what she used to be—ain't what she used to be—ain't what she used to be ..." with a great fart in the appropriate place together with the action as Dad pointed his backside at the audience. A bit rude, maybe, but the military audience lapped it up. And the audience always called for his Stanley Holloway monologue of "Sam—Sam—pick up tha musket." Dad was near professional with monologues.

Night-time was the worst part of being on board ship. We hated sleeping in our clothes with our lifebelts over the top. To add to the discomfort, we could hear the engines forever throbbing away, the bawling of babies and people continually stumbling to toilets. We had many disturbed nights.

Lifeboat drill took place every day, soon accepted as a way of life and carried out, party fashion, in high spirits—until we were told by loudspeaker that the drill we had just completed was in fact the real thing. Submarines had been sighted but driven off by our naval escort. After this announcement, lifeboat drill was viewed much more seriously, at least on the part of the grown-ups.

So one day followed another, with Mum becoming more and more harassed as the journey went one. Five children to feed, clothe and watch all of the time gnawed away at her patience and temper. There were no longer any servants to handle all of the chores, and Father was absent most of the time—for army routines continued as normal, even on board ship.

It must have been both a surprise and a great relief when our troopship docked at Marseilles on January 4th 1940, exactly three weeks to the day from leaving Bombay. It was considered too dangerous to sail on through the Atlantic to a British port as the sea lanes were infested with German submarines, so the Regiment was disembarked and entrained for the two day journey to Cherbourg. Two Channel steamers took us on to Southampton, where, in true British fashion, the travel-weary families were subjected to a detailed and lengthy customs' inspection.

A cold and overcast January day saw the families lined up on the quayside with their baggage and bedrolls in front of them. We seemed to wait for ages as the customs men worked through the long lines of families.

The Regiment had over five hundred and forty officers and men, a figure to be trebled with wives and children.

I noticed that Mum had put on weight and Dad was whispering to her now and again. The family was freezing as we flapped our hands about trying to keep warm.

At last the customs men were talking to Dad.

'Anything to declare, sergeant?'

'No, sir, nothing at all.'

The men chalked a couple of bags and were about to move on when one said, 'Open that bedroll, sergeant.'

Dad calmly unbuckled the leather straps and rolled out the canvas bedroll. Pillows, blankets—nothing else. The customs men moved on. It wasn't until later we learnt that Father had filled all his pillows with tea and carefully restitched the ends. Mother, for

49

her part, had yards of Indian silk wound round her body under her dress. No wonder they were whispering, but all ended well.

We were then put on trains again and arrived in the Garrison at Colchester on the following morning, January 7th 1940. We had experienced days of chaotic travel from a temperature of one hundred and twenty degrees in the shade, to minus two on the cold, damp day when we eventually rolled into Colchester Barracks and off-loaded once more from lorries. Now Mother will get some peace, I thought, a home like other people. God, she deserved it after what she had been through.

The first night we spent in the garrison gymnasium, supposedly while the married quarters were sorted out. This never happened, because there were many more families than there were quarters. Consequently some were boarded out in civilian accommodation and we were allocated temporary quarters in an army block that had not been used for some time. It was a three storey building in a poor state of repair and we had the bottom flat. Mum and Dad did their best to make it habitable.

On my birthday, January 18th, a neighbour hurried round to the flat to tell us that she had just heard Mum's name read out on the wireless. In those days they broadcast what they called S.O.S. messages. Apparently Mum's mother was at death's door in a hospital in Worcester. Mum immediately got on a train. She told the story years later of arriving at the Worcester hospital and being told by the staff that her mother had been expected to pass away each day for over three weeks but had been clinging to life, all the time asking for her.

Mum was an only child and we had never heard her speak of her father. When she married Fred, her mother was a widow. Mum had written regularly to my grandmother while we were in India but had not had time to visit her since our return to England. Now she entered the Dickensian ward to find her mother propped up on some pillows, black shawl around her shoulders, eyes closed. It was late at night and only a single bulb threw sparse light over the sleeping patients. As Mum kissed her, Grandma's eyes opened and a faint smile touched the corners of her mouth.

'I knew you would come,' she said, in a whisper. There was a long silence. Then, in a voice as faint as a breath she said, 'That's all I've been waiting for,' and her fingers tightened on Mum's hand as she peacefully died—still with a wisp of a smile on her pale, careworn face.

Our dismal, damp quarters became damper still when the area all the way round the married quarters was flooded. For two days we couldn't leave the flat. Father came in that evening and added to Mother's problems by saying he had been posted to Fort Knox, in America, on a course to become an instructor on tanks.

The Americans, although not yet in the war, were supplying military hardware to Britain. Father would be leaving in about four weeks and decided to resettle the family in Worcester, where most of his brothers lived. It was also Mum's home town. No doubt the idea was his family would keep an eye on and help us. Father did not know how long he would be away, but arranged immediate leave to sort things out.

Somehow, he also arranged to borrow a lorry and a couple of troopers. The family's few bits of furniture were loaded and we took off once more; this time to a new strange life at Martley, deep in the heart of the Worcester countryside.

7

FATHER CAME FROM A LARGE FAMILY of twelve children and was born at Broadwas, in Worcestershire. Most of his brothers worked on the land, some as private gardeners to big houses. There was one exception. Uncle Frank, two years older than Dad, was a roadman for the council.

Frank lived at the village of Martley, in "The Forge," a bungalow that still had the one-time village smithy attached to it. The smithy's worn brick floor was now the home of some bicycles (everyone had a bike); boxes, stacked in great piles storing the summer's fruits, mostly apples and plums; strings of onions hung up to dry and removed one at a time, as needed, by Auntie Em, Frank's wife; piles of logs for winter warmth; oil cans; old bicycle wheels; tyres; kindling wood; and some items that would fetch a fortune in today's market, including a brass knobbed iron bedstead. The smell in the smithy was marvellous, as the aroma of apples, onions, leatherwork and logs mingled and matured. Frank and Em, with daughter, Eileen, had lived at The Forge for many years and were well respected in the area.

It was Frank who found us the cottage, just half a mile away on the road out to Martley Post Office and crossroads. It was a farm cottage that hadn't been occupied for a couple of years, but it looked lovely after what we had been used to, and I felt sure we had found a real home at last. It stood on its own, facing onto a B road, the nearest building being the village shop some one hundred yards up the hill.

The front door of the cottage led directly into a small front room and a scullery/kitchen type leanto was attached to the back of the house. There were two ten foot square identical bedrooms and, to the rear, a small yard housed an outside privvy—a two seater—and a rusty old pump that didn't work. There was no electricity, so oil lamps and candles were acquired from the shop.

52

Beyond the yard was a big meadow with a backcloth of grassy hills and, in the centre of the meadow, a small copse of trees with a pond surrounded by an iron fence. This picturesque setting was to offer peace and happiness to us all, I sincerely hoped.

We arrived at the cottage after picking up Uncle Frank and Auntie Em from their bungalow. They had obviously been here before, as a path had been cut to the front door through four foot high stinging nettles and the whole place had been swept out and windows cleaned. With all helping, our few bits of furniture were soon unloaded and Father took Vic and me up the hill to the shop for the first of many visits to fetch pails of drinking water.

We all rattled around in the house that first evening, every footstep echoing on the bare floorboards in the dim atmosphere of one ancient oil lamp and candles in saucers. The chimney hadn't been swept and the open fire puffed woodsmoke into the living-room. The soldiers slept downstairs with Father, as Vic, John and I lay head to tail, three in a bed, upstairs, giggling and excited in our new surroundings. A sharp word from Father came up the stairs and silence reigned.

Dad and his lorry took off early for Worcester and returned at midday with more furniture acquired at a secondhand shop, after which the lorry and soldiers drove off back to Colchester, leaving Father to settle his family into their new surrounding. Of all the new furniture, the pine-timbered, black-legged, square kitchen table was the item I remember best. It was used for everything from feeding the family and ironing to rolling out pastry. It was scrubbed daily and was perfectly white. Mother covered it with newspaper at meal-times until she bought a piece of red and white check oilcloth. I often had the job of scraping pastry from between the gaps in the planks when Mother finished baking. The table travelled everywhere with the family for years to come.

The one luxury that came into the house that day early in 1940 was a wireless. It was nearly three feet high and eighteen inches in depth. It ran on an acid accumulator and an HT battery. Dad bought two accumulators as they only lasted two days and then had to be taken to the village shop to be recharged. Much pleasure was had by the family on dark winter evenings listening to this amazing invention.

Mornings we regularly awoke to the sound of cockerels crowing and cows mooing, no longer the trumpeter playing reveille or the hustle and bustle of an army camp. Everything felt strange and quiet, but very exciting.

At breakfast we sat round our new secondhand table. Dad had a side to himself, Mum sat to his left, next to baby Pauline in her clumsy, wooden highchair, Ernie and John to the right and me and Vic facing Father. How excited we were in our new dream home. We just couldn't wait to go out exploring.

'You must have water, Vi; you can't manage otherwise,' said Dad. 'I'll take Vic and Bob after breakfast to see if I can get the old pump working.'

I looked at Vic and he looked at me with glum face, hunching his shoulders. Exploring would have to wait. I couldn't imagine how Dad thought he could mend an old, rusty pump—it seemed a daft idea to me.

The village shop loaned Dad a few more buckets after he explained to the shopkeeper what he intended to do.

'"Prime it," you say, Fred? Sounds a tall order. Must be two years since Albert left that cottage,' said the shopkeeper. 'Mind you, it worked then all right.'

With encouraging words, dad lifted a full bucket in each hand and set off the hundred yards downhill to the cottage saying, 'Come on, lads, the sooner we get it working, the better.'

With three quarters of a bucketful each we sloshed down the hill behind him. Both of us had wet socks and shoes before we reached the pump. Ah well, I thought, if a couple of buckets of water is all it takes to get a pump working it will be well worth it.

For the next three days we crawled, ached and stumbled up and down the hill, while an obstinate but determined Father carried his buckets with hardly a break. The water was poured down the top of the pump and Father was sure that once fully primed it would start working. We thought it was a mad idea yet we didn't dare say so and every few hours he pumped away on the handle but nothing happened.

Mother watched and worried about her two boys but Dad would not be persuaded to give up. Arms and legs aching, the ridiculous fiasco continued and after the third day of endlessly carrying water and pumping the handle without success, Mother finally had her way. It was decided to forget the pump and we reverted to only filling buckets and the tin bath for our daily wants. In the second week, Mother trooped us all down to Martley village to start at the village school.

Whereas Vic was the strong one of the family and I was the

skinny bean pole, and both of us were noisy, inquisitive, confident and outgoing, brother John was the opposite.

John had a lovely face, lighter skinned than us two; his hair was also lighter. His eyes were pale blue and set perfectly in a well proportioned face with paper thin, almost female lips. Vic's face was square, my face was long and pointed but John's was beautifully crafted. He was the quiet one, never taking the initiative, always ready to join in once Vic or I had decided what to do. He already showed leanings towards being artistic and outshone both of us when it came to drawing lessons at Martley school. Although Mother loved each and every one of us, I do believe that John had a special place in her heart.

The school was typical of its time, built of grey stone blocks with a slate roof and high-ceilinged classrooms. There were only fourteen pupils in the whole school, so our arrival caused quite a stir and the three of us soon settled in. It was just over two miles from our cottage, mostly across fields.

The teacher was a lovely old lady, with silver hair in a bun, a lovely pink complexion and smiling, understanding, soft eyes. We liked her immediately. Sandwiches were taken for lunch and a small bottle of milk was supplied by the school to each pupil. So Mum got some respite having only Ernie and baby Pauline to look after.

With the help of Uncle Frank, Father cleared the stinging nettles from both sides of the cottage, and various fruit trees, old rabbit hutches and a lovely copse were all now accessible. His leave was fast running out but he found time to take the family on walks in the area. Many happy memories remain of those lanes, hills and fields where Dad would use his army knife, which he always carried, to cut a three foot straight stick from the hedgerow and a smaller three inch piece with a knot in it. He then taught us how to play "tippet-and-run": the one who flicked the three inch piece the longest distance with the three foot stick was the winner, for whom he could always produce a boiled sweet. The losers also got a sweet each, so everyone was happy.

Dad knew a great deal about nature and would collect leaves and challenge us to name the trees they had come from—boiled sweets again. The family—especially us boys and Father—came much closer together during this time and I responded by keeping out of trouble.

It was soon the very last weekend before the end of Dad's leave and he decided to have one more go at the pump. We were all well known at the shop by then. Our daily visits for water or accumulator charging, or more often for an extra loaf of bread, seemed to give us preference over any other customer.

The shopkeeper looked at him and his two boys in disbelief as Dad explained. 'I've just got to get that pump going. I can't leave Violet without water if I can help it. Bad enough leaving her on her own with five young-uns.'

Vic and I were resigned to the fact that Father was crazy and we would be carrying buckets all week-end until he went back off leave. In the event we had done no more than a dozen trips and were halfway back to the house when we heard his excited voice wafting up the hill.

'Vi, Vi, come and look; it's working.'

We left our buckets and ran the rest of the way to the yard to find him furiously pumping water all over the yard. We all learnt another lesson that day: never give in. Dad had succeeded when we thought he was mad.

We all saw him off on the Midland Red bus from Martley Post Office. We didn't know when we would see him again. Poor Mother, left with five young children, miles from Worcester, a war on, ration books and an army allowance of only three pounds sixteen shillings payable at the post office on Saturdays to provide for us all. She put on a brave face as we gathered round Pauline's pram for the two mile trek back to the cottage. We weren't to know about Mother being pregnant again, or indeed the tragedies that were to befall us in the next few months.

My Mum was a marvellous person who doted on her five offspring. It was a busy life for her after her years in India with servants to do all the work. The house was cold when we got up in the mornings and she had to light the fire, prepare breakfast and make up sandwiches, all in time to get us off to school before she could catch her breath. Vic and I had not only to dress and get ourselves ready for school, but also help John to get ready, and dress Ernie.

We three eldest boys left the cottage each day at eight-thirty for school and I well remember Mum, standing at the gate with Ernie and baby Pauline, giving her orders.

'Straight to school now, no playing on the way and don't eat

56

your sandwiches until lunchtime,' this last part of daily routine orders directed with a knowing smile towards Vic.

So much for weekdays, then came Saturday, shopping day, the most exciting day of the week.

The same ritual was carried out every Saturday. The whole family—Pauline in her high sprung Swallow pram with Ernie sitting on the end, legs dangling—trekked down to Martley Post Office where Mum got her allowance and caught the nine-fifty Midland Red bus to Worcester. She took Pauline and Ernie with her while we three boys pushed the pram back to the cottage.

The little lecture before the bus left was always the same. 'Look after John and don't get into any mischief. The soup's in the pan for lunch and be here when the bus gets back at ten past four.' Kiss, kiss, kiss.

As the bus disappeared, so the pram accelerated. It was a marvellous toy to Vic and me. With John reluctantly placed inside, the pram zig-zagged and dirt-tracked from one side of the narrow road to the other, screams coming from a pair of legs flaying the air, as the pram made record time home.

We amused ourselves in various ways during the day and sometimes I used to take off on my own, exploring. Great excitement came when it was time to meet the bus. We hoped that Mother would have goodies for us all, and she never disappointed us.

As we walked back from the bus with her, Pauline buried under shopping bags in the pram and Ernie trying to keep up, we stuffed our mouths with chocolate bars and biscuits, which were still available in that first year of the war. We always enjoyed this feast and came to accept that by Tuesday or Wednesday of the following week the cupboard would be bare. For all my Mum's good points, and she was a loving mother, she could not manage her money and it was "bread and scrape" from midweek to Saturday payday.

I found many ways to pass the time on those Saturdays; a favourite was chasing the cows in the meadow behind the cottage. Once they were running fast I had them going in circles round the fenced-off copse and pond. Mother was not aware of this hobby until one evening the local policeman called. It appeared that one of the cows in the back meadow had dropped dead and one of her boys had been seen chasing them. I received a dire warning from the stern policeman who put the fear of God into me, and I gave up this particular pastime for good. It was either that, I was told, or

I'd be taken away from my family.

One Saturday some weeks later, while seeing Mum off on the morning bus we noticed Uncle Frank's road repair lorry in the village, outside the school. Uncle Frank was a friendly fellow and always had mischief in his eyes; he was still a child at heart and loved to play pranks on people. He liked us boys and was always a good touch for a thruppenny bit. He had a zest for living.

When Dad was home we had visited the forge one night. Frank always sat in his old armchair to the left of the big, black-leaded fire grate, smoking his Star cigarettes and spitting into the fire. He would let off a rasping fart and shout "rabbits!" and then point his imaginary gun round the room shouting, "bang-bang."

We laughed so much, and his eyes were watery lights of mischievous happiness, as Auntie Em shot out of the scullery, smiles all over her lovely round face and admonished Frank saying, 'Frank, not in front of the children,' but even she loved to see her house full of happy people and enjoyed Frank's broad, earthy fun as much as we did.

After taking the pram back to the cottage and eating our soup early we decided to find Uncle Frank's road repair gang and offer our help. He was delighted to see us and gave us a few menial tasks to do, and in no time at all we were covered in tar. Our shoes, knees, hands and, in my case, my face all had tar on them at which I'd had a good scratch. Frank obviously decided we were in enough mess, so he gave us tuppence each and we dashed off to the post office for goodies.

It was now two hours before Mum returned on the bus and we tried to remove the tar with dockleaves and grass but to no avail. We ran back to Uncle Frank and asked him what to do.

'Cow muck,' said Frank, 'that's the stuff to get it off,' and gullible as we were, we made for the fields and furiously rubbed cow muck over the tar, with gales of laughter and much pinching of noses. Mother regaled family friends years later of the sight that greeted her as she stepped down off the Midland Red that Saturday in March 1940, and of course it became one of Frank's favourite stories.

Tragedy struck a few weeks later while Mum was at Worcester shopping. I was upstairs when I heard Vic's voice shouting from the front garden. 'Bob, Bob, the house is on fire.'

How it happened was never established but on fire it was, and I found heavy smoke coming up the narrow, fully enclosed steep stairway.

Without a second thought I opened the bedroom window, perched on the window sill for a moment, then jumped the ten feet to the weedy grass below. It was fear that drove me to do it and fortune favours the brave; I was uninjured but very frightened. John was with Vic and we made for the nearest refuge—the shop.

The flames took a good hold of the cottage and nothing could be done to contain them as we were so isolated from any form of assistance. When the fire had burnt itself out we were left with half a cottage and the smell of damp wood everywhere. Mother was very upset but thankful we were all right.

The Army was informed and after a few days of Mum and the two youngest trying to live in half of the cottage, and us three boys living at the Forge with Frank and Em, we moved yet again, this time to the village of Suckley.

8

THE HUGE VICTORIAN MANOR HOUSE at Suckley stood in acres of its own grounds and was owned and occupied by a widow, Mrs Taylor-Simpson. She was a lady straight out of the Victorian era: always impeccably dressed, silver grey hair surrounding her sombre face, and definitely superior to all she surveyed. She didn't take kindly to having an army family billeted on her. There were servants in the house and a gamekeeper named Alec.

We moved with practically no furniture except for the faithful kitchen table which had miraculously survived, and were allocated the trophy room over the stables in the yard. No doubt there were spare bedrooms galore in the manor house itself and Mrs Simpson must have been rattling around like a pea in a drum, but the Freeman's station in life did not fit them for such gracious living.

We set up temporary beds in the trophy room, thirty feet long with a polished wood floor, and were to be watched over by antlers, mooses' heads, a bear's head, and glass enclosed reptiles for the next couple of months. Mother bought a two foot by one foot tin paraffin cooker, a tin kettle and a baking pan. This was the sum of her catering equipment for feeding her brood and she could only cook in small quantities.

The Lady of the Manor extended her generosity on our first day there by sending a message, via her maid, that a meal would be ready at five o'clock if we reported to the rear door. This we did, and ate our sausages and mash in the large kitchen, which inspired awe and silence. That was the only treat we were ever to receive from her.

The big house was set back on a hillside, well off the narrow C road. A long, winding, tree-lined drive crossed a small bridge and a stream and climbed a low hill to the front door. A path branched round to the left to a courtyard and stables. The nearest shop was three miles away and poor Mother pushed her pram almost daily to and from the village in spite of her advancing pregnancy.

We started at yet another school—on top of a hill next to the church, over two miles for us to walk daily with no short cuts across fields. Vic and I also joined the church choir and, on alternate Sundays, took our turn at pumping the organ instead of singing. Great fun was achieved by winning a dare to let the organ run short of air in the middle of a hymn. Then, by pumping like mad, a great farting noise could be achieved and a few pennies earned off the other choirboys for doing so.

The gamekeeper, Alec, was a smashing chap and became a real friend of the family. He would often take me and Vic with him on his tour of the estate. We were taught to smoke out rabbits, by first studying the rabbit families while concealed for long periods behind brambles or trees. Alec established which burrows were in use, and pegged all but one of them securely with sacks, ensuring that all holes were covered. The one left open was always facing the prevailing wind. Next, he lit a fire over the open hole and when it was going well, covered it with damp foliage. The smoke was wafted down the hole into the maze of burrows below the ground. Eventually the rabbits ran for it, straight into the dark mouths of the sacks. The gamekeeper was skilled at this procedure, though he sometimes had to send his ferret down on the end of a long string if the smoke didn't work. We all benefited and became quite fond of rabbit stew.

In the following weeks, while Mother struggled on, we enjoyed life in the country as only children can at that age, with total freedom to fill their ample spare time.

Vic and I had been earning a few shillings helping on the local farms. Hay making was still done by hand and with half a loaf, a great lump of the farmer's cheese and a bottle of cold, sweet tea each, we spent many weekends turning the grass to dry and, days later, pitch-forking it on to the horse-drawn carts. Fruit and tater picking came later when all the family joined in.

Hop picking was by far the best and most memorable experience and Mum was very fast at it. She had a crib of her own and we boys had half-size cribs. It was exciting, because all the local families were in the hop fields with their children and, as there was only one school, everybody knew one another. The picking season was always towards the end of the school's six week summer holiday and was an opportunity to earn big money.

The mornings were often cold and misty as the families arrived

61

early in the hop field. A big fire was lit and all babies in prams were put to windward of it. The farmer would then allocate cribs and a farmhand would start cutting down the twelve foot high vines, bottom first. Off everybody went, pulling the lovely shaped hop cones from the vines, at the same time, trying not to pick any leaves. Chatter and singing started as the sun began to shine and everybody seemed so happy. The children were picking into their small cribs. Every hour the farmer would come along with a big bushel basket and empty each crib, shouting out the number of bushels as he emptied the contents into his farmhand's sacks. The number of bushels scooped out of each crib was recorded by the farm clerk and fourpence per bushel would be paid out, in cash, at the end of the day.

Woe betide anyone with too many leaves in their crib, for they would be passed over by the farmer until the leaves had been removed. Hearty banter and leg pulling went on between the happy farmer and his female pickers.

The families stopped for lunch, the black kettle was placed over the open fire and we all sat round it on sacks eating ravenously. Whatever we had to eat, usually sandwiches, had to be held between newspaper, as our fingers were stained black from the hops and anything that we touched was tainted with bitterness, but this in no way affected the lovely happy atmosphere of those hop picking days.

Mother's pregnancy was well advanced by now. She was nearly eight months gone, but she still kept happy. It was almost six months since Dad had left; many letters had been sent and received but still we weren't sure when he was going to return. The first Saturday in September 1940, almost a year from the war's commencement, came round.

Mum had gone down to the village pushing the ever present pram—which doubled as a shopping trolley—with Pauline and Ernie. Vic and I were left to our own devices—and to look after brother John. Suddenly we missed him. We started to search and call his name. No John anywhere.

'Perhaps he's gone after Mother,' said Vic, so we went down from the courtyard along the winding drive shouting his name and were passing over the hump-backed little bridge.

I don't remember who noticed what first, but I retain the most vivid and horrific memory of seeing John lying face-up in the water below. His hands were outstretched, palms upwards and his face was just below the water, his eyes staring. His feet were stuck in the thick mud churned up by the many cattle that used the stream. The water was only three feet deep.

How long we stood there I cannot remember, only that I eventually took off at great speed to find Mother, and Vic ran to find the gamekeeper, Alec.

Mother was totally distraught as she rushed back through the lanes with the three of us. Someone had sent for the local policeman, who arrived just before Aunty Em and Uncle Frank. Everybody did what they could in the circumstances, but poor Mother suffered terribly.

One can imagine her grief, having trekked with her family across India and survived the dangers of the North West Frontier and submarine infested seas, only to see a son drown in a shallow stream with no husband at hand to support her in this terrible time.

We older boys felt so helpless; there was nothing we could do to comfort her.

John was laid out in the big house. Mrs Taylor-Simpson showed great sympathy and understanding during this dreadful period and came down from her house to the trophy room.

'I'm sure you would like to see your brother John—come along, I'll take you,' she said to me and Vic, holding her hands out in friendly gesture.

I didn't really know what she meant and I wasn't sure I wanted to see John now he was dead. But I was also too frightened to say "No" to the grand lady.

Vic and I were led across the paved area around the house, which, only the previous week, she had employed us to weed all day for thruppence. We entered the big house at the front door for the first time and I was immediately frightened by the sheer size of the hall and height of the ceiling. I seemed that much smaller and lost the secure feeling of always being hemmed in by walls.

She led us up the biggest stairway I'd ever seen, then down a dim-lit corridor, passing a number of solid, dark oak doors.

At last she opened a door into a large bedroom. The curtains were drawn, but the lights were on. My eyes immediately went to the large four-poster bed in the centre of the long wall opposite. There lay John, slightly propped up on his pillow. He looked like an angel. His face was beautifully clean, shiny and white, although he had cotton wool in his nostrils which I couldn't understand at the time. His hair had been brushed neatly and he was wearing a clean night-shirt. They had crossed his hands in front of him on the turnover piece of white sheet, and someone had made a nice pattern of fresh daisies around his hands and on his pillow. He looked at peace with the world, as truly he was.

I was glad to have this picture as my last memory of him and not the nightmare remembrance of him in the stream. My heart was full of sorrow then, as it is today, when I wonder what else I might have done to save my nearest brother.

John was buried in Suckley churchyard. No headstone marked his grave; I suppose no money was available. I returned, years later, but could only stand in the approximate place and say my prayer for him. Dad arrived home for the funeral and we were pleased Mum had someone to lean on at last.

'You can't stay here, Vi,' he said that first night. 'I'll see if I can find another place tomorrow.'

Two days later Father came back from Worcester on the Midland Red bus and told us all he had arranged to rent a house there.

'Right next to the Cathedral, Vi and five minutes from the Shambles.' The Shambles being the main shopping area in Worcester. But this did little to cheer Mother up.

We packed again, said our farewells to Mrs Taylor-Simpson and dear old Alec and set off on our lorry for Worcester.

Father stayed on for another week, but eventually couldn't get any more compassionate leave. However, he did manage to get us fairly settled in the great barn of a place he had found for us.

It was a three-storey terraced house, cold and damp with no view at the back but a brick wall. Access to the upper floors was by way of a steep and narrow boarded-in stairway. There was no electricity so once more the oil-lamps and candles came out.

We were all suffering from the loss of John and Mother wasn't capable of doing much. Vic and I were sent out shopping for most things. Mum provided the list of wants and I always remember her saying, 'Don't forget to ask for yesterday's bread.' Yesterday's bread was always half price.

Another duty was pushing an old high-sprung pram, false bottom removed, to the gas works right across Worcester close to the sauce factory. We returned with the pram full of coke, and often the man who filled it up took pity on the two scruffy boys and gave us a penny back out of sixpence.

We survived a few more weeks; Vic and I did all we could to

help Mum. We weren't put to school during this period and spent most of the time around the house or running errands.

Mother went into hospital and Dad was sent for again. Baby Graham was born, the seventh Freeman. Mum came home and we all hoped the new baby would take her mind off losing John.

On the sixth day of Mum's homecoming I was lying in bed with Vic on the first floor. It was early and the dawn was just breaking when I woke with a start.

Mum was screaming, 'Fred, Fred, he's not breathing.'

We rushed downstairs in our shirt-tails to see Father, with Graham in his arms and holding tight to poor, hysterical Mother.

Graham was dead. 'Perforated lungs at birth,' said the doctors.

We cried for John, we cried again for Graham. If there was a God, how could he treat us in this way? Mother, understandably, could take no more and became very ill.

Mother's illness was prolonged and it was decided the family had to be split up. Whereas some could go to Uncle and Aunt's it was reluctantly agreed that I, the unruly one, should go to military boarding school.

I lay in bed with Vic; our bedroom was directly over the front room and I heard Father talking to Mother.

'It's no good, Vi, he's uncontrollable, we can't possibly board him out with a relative. The Army boarding school's the only place for him. Discipline, that's what he needs.'

Poor Mother, as if she hadn't suffered enough, now she was to lose her family. There was no arguing with Father that night.

At that point in time I wanted to run away but the fear of the unknown world and being alone was greater than the fear of being taken from my mother. Pleading and crying had no affect on Father as I was dragged off to the railway station.

And so fate decreed that I should be abandoned at Saunton Sands, near Braunton in Devon where I became a "newchie" a boy soldier at the Duke of York's Royal Military School.

Never to see my Mother, brothers or sister for the next two years, and to spend five years surviving amongst three hundred and sixty boys and archaic, bullying regimes. I had many more lessons to learn. Most of them the hard way.

9

CAVERNOUS, HOLLOW, EMPTY, UNFRIENDLY, but most of all *cold*. Poorly lit, echoing, ghostly, frightening . . . Saunton Sands Hotel 1941.

Fear of the unknown, helplessness and panic gripped me as Father said his goodbyes to C.S.M. Halyard and me. I pleaded to go back with Dad, my tears and anguish to no avail.

I was left with this strange man, in this strange cold place, frightened and trembling. Father's back disappeared into the night. I bit my lip as warm tears dropped off my face. Abandoned.

C.S.M. Halyard took me up three flights of rubber-covered stairs and down an ill-lit corridor. The sparsely spaced bulbs threw circles of pale light on the cream gloss walls. Low murmurings could be heard as we passed darkened rooms with no doors. I followed the big uniformed man in front of me, almost running to keep up with his stride, frightened that I lose him, my only contact with the world. I was nine years old.

We entered a hole in the wall and he showed me my top bunk for my first night's sleep with the "Dukies."

'Get yourself to bed, son, and I'll see you in the morning,' he whispered, giving me a flannelette nightshirt.

It was late at night, after lights out, and the hole in the wall where the door used to be was just a grey patch in the blackness. I could hear a boy sobbing and feel eyes looking at me as I shakily undressed and climbed up into my hard, cold top bunk. Silence.

I lay under my bedclothes—utterly distraught—and let my pent-up feeling take over. I had no control as my body convulsed with emotion, yearning for someone, anyone, to comfort me.

Cast into a cold, unfriendly, strange and fearful world, a world that offered no promise, no hand to hold, no ear to listen, no friend, no mother, no family. Alone, afraid, helpless, a piece of flotsam on a heaving sea, all that was life—gone. I truly felt nobody cared about me, nobody cared whether I lived or died. I thought of my brother John and baby Graham, whose tragic end had split up our family. I loved my mother dearly and my brothers and sister, yes, even Father, and because of this love I couldn't understand why they'd abandoned me after all we'd been through together. I wanted to die.

To truly appreciate and enjoy great heights of happiness, one must have experienced great painful depths of sadness. Indeed, to achieve contentment one must travel the opposite road, sometimes, almost without hope.

Such was my view of life at that moment—without hope.

I was to travel on alone, no mother in time of trouble, no goodnight kiss, no brothers or sister. Further down the desolate road was my destiny. For the first time I had no-one to run to, no-one to comfort me, no refuge. Not yet ten years old and cast out into the strange world of a boy's military boarding school. I cried my body dry.

That first night—a living nightmare that still occasionally haunts me when a scene on TV or a few words in a book rub against the raw wound in my memory—eventually came to an end. I was aware of a trumpeter sounding reveille. My confused thoughts flashed me to York Barracks, India, Colchester Barracks, all in a second. Then as I came to I realised where I actually was. Fear re-entered my body.

Scared faces of other boys peered above their bed clothes. We lay there wondering who we were, where we were, and what was going to happen to us. We didn't have to wait long.

'On your feet newchies—on your feet—NOW!'

The loud and frightening command came from a podgy, fat faced boy who I disliked immediately. His short, dark wavy hair was parted down the middle of his large head and his glaring eyes were hardly an inch apart. He grabbed a handful of bedclothes from a bottom bunk bed and pulled them roughly away leaving the terrified occupant shivering with fear. All boys were on the floor in an instant. 'Get washed, dressed and bedding folded for C.S.M.'s inspection in ten minutes—MOVE!'

Sure enough, ten minutes later, we were washed and roughly dressed, but our beds were still in disarray, when the C.S.M. entered followed by the piggy eyed fat boy.

'Ah—the new boys' dormitory—Good morning boys' said the C.S.M. in a soft gentle voice. No- one could summoned up a reply.

'I'm your Company Sergeant Major—you'll be seeing a lot of me. Pinder here is the House Senior Boy and he will take you to breakfast. I'll see you after Assembly. Carry on Pinder.'

Breakfast . . . the strange and forbidding dining hall, the atmosphere and the sheer number of boys drained me of hunger.

I gazed round the rows of long tables, each seating twenty four—twelve a side—as the single files of noisy boys pushed, shoved and scrambled to their allotted places.

'There, there and there,' grunted Pinder indicating places on the long forms. 'That's where you'll always sit till I tell you different.'

We slid into our places and became the focus of all eyes—the newchies had arrived. The eyes knew what our fate was to be, we didn't.

A shrill whistle brought immediate silence, all attention focused on the duty C.S.M who surveyed the dining hall.

'We give thanks, O Lord, for our daily bread and are ever mindful of those less fortunate,' sang the bespectacled Chaplain.

'Amen,' chanted the boys.

The whole dining hall then erupted with noise. Eager conversations were punctuated with the clatter of hurrying feet and shouts of instruction as three big boys from the bottom of each row of tables made a dash for the servery. They returned with large steel containers of lumpy, pale scrambled egg swimming in water and another container of half slices of fried bread.

The first few plates were loaded with more than generous portions and passed, hand to hand, up the table to Pinder and his friends. My appetite was returning as I viewed the crisp fried bread passing in front of me. Then I noticed as each successive plate was passed along the table, from willing hand to willing hand, that the portions became progressively smaller until the newchies' plates arrived with only a quarter slice of fried bread and a derisory amount of watery egg. My first lesson was then registered, we, the newchies were crap, nonentities, with no rights or voice, bottom of the pile again.

The three of us, still strangers but in the same boat, looked at one another in disappointment. I looked up the long table towards Pinder who was sitting on a chair at the head of the table. He was watching us and our eyes met. He grinned at his friends then turned back to us.

'No talking. Get on with your food.'

Our christening breakfast and entry into the dining hall ritual had begun.

After breakfast we were delivered, by Pinder, to the C.S.M and Matron who were waiting for us in the storeroom next to the surgery.

'Well done, Pinder,' said the C.S.M. 'Now you get about your business.'

'Yes sir,' clipped Pinder with a smile of self-importance.

We were then told to undress, even in front of Matron, and stood there like three little skeletons while clothes were selected off the racks.

First a white vest, then a hairy khaki shirt without a collar, underpants, a pair of short khaki trousers with a nice crease at the front of each leg, long brown knee length stockings, big heavy black boots, a khaki tunic with brass buttons and clips to the "dog collar" neck, and last of all a forage cap. Within fifteen minutes the three new soldier boys were born.

'There now—you do look a treat,' the Matron said kindly

'Yes, they certainly do Matron. Come along boys, let's get started, you'll soon get the hang of things once you've made a few friends. You're all going to be bandsmen—how do you like that?'

We nervously followed the C.S.M. in our heavy clothes, stumbling behind him in the uncomfortably stiff boots that almost refused to be lifted off the floor. It was like learning to walk again.

The C.S.M. was a kindly man who took the time to show us the locations of those places we immediately had to know; our classroom, the band room, the gymnasium, the main assembly hall—originally the hotel ballroom—and of course the parade ground.

The three storey, rectangular hotel now requisitioned for Army use, was somewhat isolated, three miles from Braunton, the nearest village, and set on the top of tall cliffs, with spectacular and uninterrupted views across many miles of Saunton Sands and Bideford Bay. But it was too early for us to appreciate the wonderful views.

Those first few strange mornings came as a shock to the system. No longer casually waking and leisurely dressing with Mum's voice in the background chivvying me on. No longer the family breakfast and a full stomach, with a homely atmosphere, familiarity and security.

Once reveille sounded there was a mad panicky rush for a cold wash, often three or more to a tap. Then quickly donning our bulky uniform, ton-heavy boots and forage cap, we plunged in a mad stampede down three flights of stairs; out through the vestibule to the sloping car park and paraded in companies in the cold light of dawn, panting with fright. Roll call followed as we stood and shivered. Then we set off marching through the country lanes for forty minutes. After this hectic start to the day, breakfast came as a relief, although we invariably left the table for our first school lessons feeling just as hungry as when we'd entered the dining hall.

Three sessions followed in our hutted classrooms at the front of the hotel which had views across the cliff tops to five miles of beautiful sandy beach, lashing seas and the backdrop of Bideford Bay. Then came an hour of Trade Training, in my case band practice.

Lunch followed, a painful ritual now more of a punishment than a pleasure, and the afternoons were filled either with sport—football, boxing or cross-country running—or field training and drill practice or, of course, more classroom work.

The day didn't finish then, oh no, not with three hundred and sixty boys to control! After tea there was another hour's Trade Training before you were released to your own devices.

A full day with no time to think was a blessing that went unappreciated. It was only when we finally climbed into our bunk beds that we had time to think and in those early days our thoughts were always of home. I believe I always eventually fell asleep with wet cheeks from crying softly.

It was towards the end of my first week that terror struck.

I had never imagined that anything could happen which could worsen my situation. How wrong I was!

I was being shaken. It was dark, in the middle of the night, four faces grinned at me through the gloom.

'Come with us,' they said, pulling me from my top bunk. Sheer panic gripped me.

'Where to?' I stuttered.

Great smiles and giggles—'You'll find out,' they said as I was frog-marched, trembling with fear, down the dark corridor, my feet sticking to the rubber floor.

The largest room on the top floor, which must have previously been a lounge, but was now a dormitory, was full of grinning older boys. Standing there with expressions of anticipated excitement, in their blue and white striped flannelette night shirts, they looked like miniature Caesars waiting for the Christians to be thrown to the lions; some boys were sitting on the top bunks to get a better view.

Half asleep—and shivering in cold panic, I was held in front of a table, opposite the seated fat-faced Pinder, a name etched with fear into the memory of every newchie. Still held by my arms I stood on the bare floorboards wondering if I was dreaming.

'Your name, boy?' demanded Pinder.

'Bob Freeman,' I croaked.

As I replied I let out a great scream as excruciating pain shot up my leg. Beneath the blanket covering the table one of Pinder's henchmen had brought down the heel of a boot hard onto my toes.

The room burst into laughter at this expected act in the play.

'Sir—Bob Freeman, sir—now let's try again,' he grinned.

With tears running down my face I was now held up by the henchmen.

'What's your name, boy?'

'Bob Freeman, sir,' I gasped, clenching my toes right back to my feet.

'Whose orders are obeyed without question?'

A slight, pregnant pause ensued as I wondered what the correct answer was. Was it the C.S.M.? Was it the R.S.M.? Was it this detestable boy who sat there, leaning forward in his chair, his piercing black eyes staring straight at me? The watchers started to whisper amongst themselves.

'Quick boy—I will count to five.'

'Your orders, sir.'

'Good—you're getting the message.'

'Now, boy,' said Pinder, producing a cardboard telescope. 'Put this to your eye and look over there (pointing to the end of the room), and tell me what you can see.'

I obeyed—howls of laughter from the audience—'Nothing, sir, but bunk beds.'

'Foolish boy, try the other eye.'

More howls of laughter as I put the telescope to my other eye.

I was in a terrified state and did not know what was happening.

At any moment I expected the boot heel to come down on my sore toes again. A cup of water was poured down the telescope, the room was in uproar; the boys were convulsed with laughter.

A mirror was put in front of my face to reveal two black circles, one round each eye. The boot polish at the end of the telescope had done its job. 'Take off your nightshirt,' rapped Pinder.

I hesitated; terrified. I couldn't think of anything worse than being naked in front of all these boys.

A signal must have been given as, struggling like hell, his henchmen removed my nightshirt. I was lifted high and carried through the laughing audience and unceremoniously dumped in a bath of cold water. Those that could crowded into the large, old-fashioned bathroom to witness this pitiful ceremony.

More questions followed and wrong answers were punished by holding my head under water. Half drowned, I was coughing and terrified—would this nightmare never end?

When I'd drunk pints of bath water, I was lifted back into the big room again and more boys now took part in tossing me in a blanket. Great fun was had by all in trying to get me to hit the ceiling. Each time I banged into the ceiling they chanted "one," when it didn't reach high enough they chanted "miss." The ritual continued. Two, miss, three, miss, miss, four. . . At the call of twelve all boys let go of the blanket and I landed on the wooden floor aching all over.

I was eventually put back to bed by Pinder's henchmen, a shuddering, terrified wreck and fell asleep still sobbing, totally unable to answer the questions of my room mates who had not, as yet, been initiated. And so my new life began . . .

10

THE DUKE OF YORK'S ROYAL MILITARY SCHOOL was founded in 1801 and at that time was called the Royal Military Asylum. The school was for the children of long-term soldiers, who had been maimed or died in their country's service. Special cases were considered during the war years and I was such a case.

The permanent school was built at Dover, on top of the famous white cliffs, but at this point in my life—1941—the school had just been evacuated to Saunton, in North Devon, since the Germans—who now occupied France—had begun shelling the Dover coastline. In fact, the school had received a direct hit on Roberts House but fortunately this was after it had been evacuated.

Only three hundred and sixty boys could be accommodated in the requisitioned hotel at Saunton Sands with bunk beds in every room, ten bunk beds in the largest. The remainder of the boys, approximately one hundred and fifty in number, went to Dunblane School, the Scottish equivalent of the Dukies, for the duration of the war.

I was soon introduced to my new life as a "newchie," the name given to all new boys and which remained with them for months. It was a licence for other boys to indulge their taste for childish cruelty in any way they saw fit which would escape notice or detection by those in authority. And there were many such cruelties. The newchies were a fine source of sadistic amusement and were tormented at will and degraded.

The school was run on strict military lines. It was divided into eight houses—previously companies. Each house was assigned a particular Army trade, in which all members of the house would be trained. I was enrolled in Marlborough House and given the number M34. My trade was to be a Bflat Cornet player and bandsman. The houses were named after famous British generals: Kitchener, Roberts, Wolseley, Wolfe, Marlborough *et al.*

73

The Marlborough boys were billeted on the top floor of Saunton Sands Hotel and I found myself sharing a small room with two double bunk beds in it. The room had practically no furniture as the hotel had been stripped by the owners before the Dukies' arrival. All carpets, furniture and fittings had gone, to be replaced by the few items required for basic living. The bunk beds were fashioned from three by four inch rough timber and layers of chicken wire had been nailed across the structure to support the "biscuits". These small, square, sectional mattresses, stuffed with horsehair, were used uniformly throughout all of the services in wartime. Three of them, end to end, made a mattress for the standard service bed. Ours were made up with one sheet, two blankets and a bolster for a pillow. Adult non-commissioned soldiers and airmen serving in the U.K. got a pillow but no sheet. These were reserved for the women's Services.

Our first job each morning was to fold the blankets and sheet to exact regulation size and place them on the stacked biscuits at the head of the bed, sheet neatly placed between the two blankets. Room inspection every morning was conducted by the senior boy who just happened to be Pinder, and it was the expected thing that all newchies' bedding would be knocked to the floor—'Do it again, you stupid little boy—what are you?' emphasised by the bully with a slap to one's head.

' A stupid boy, sir.'

The two bunk beds were complemented by a square table and four chairs. A wooden trunk per bunk completed the room's furnishings. In this trunk we kept our thick, khaki overcoats and our few personal possessions. Our second pair of best boots, always highly polished, was displayed on top of the trunk. Apart from a towel, toothbrush and a piece of yellow soap, we possessed little else. Clean clothes were issued every Friday.

My dormitory had a french window on to a balcony but the balcony was out of bounds. The view from the french window was fantastic: the sea and the sands. Waves broke on five miles of golden beach which stretched below the cliffs across to Bideford Bay, and there were sand dunes for miles back towards the large village of Braunton. Saunton Sands Hotel—painted in camouflage khaki and green—was situated right on top of the cliffs and thirty yards from the edge.

The day started early in the Dukies with reveille at six-thirty.

If you didn't leap out of bed you were pulled out—top bunk or

74

not. After ablutions in cold water and room inspection, it was on parade by seven and off on a pre-breakfast march, occasionally accompanied by the band. Each house had its own particular song, sung religiously during the march.

> *"Here we are again, happy as can be*
> *all good pals and jolly good company.*
> *Never mind the weather, never mind the rain,*
> *as long as we're together, here we go again.*
> *La de dah de dah—la de dah de dee*
> *All good pals and jolly good company"*

we quavered. It was far from the truth. It didn't exactly sum up my feelings in the first few weeks at Saunton, but it was the growing friendship of Joe and Alf, the other two newchies that helped to sustain me.

We were all to suffer the same indignities of bullying, loneliness and hunger. The bond grew stronger as days passed into weeks. Our confidence started to return and Alf, a cockney boy, shared the same sense of humour as I did which was sometimes a help but often our downfall.

Breakfast over, school lessons began. The classrooms were temporary wooden huts with gabled roofs erected on the old putting green. They contained minimum furniture as befitted the time: thirty school desks, a single free-standing blackboard, and the teacher's desk with, of course, a long bamboo cane laid across it. No notice boards, displays or decoration. The floor was bare boards.

I struggled in most lessons and was often tail-end Charlie in exams. I suppose this was to be expected. The school staff were all from the army, the masters from the education corps. Many of the masters had some sort of chip on their shoulder and applied strict discipline in the classes.

One of the lessons I really enjoyed was map reading and the use of the prismatic compass. Sgt "Beaker" Parker was a good teacher but subject to quite unpredictable and often alarming mood swings.

We were comfortably into the lesson one day when he stopped mid sentence, lifted his long pointed nose in the air and inhaled slowly through his nostrils. We watched his long quivering "beak" —the source of his nickname—with curiosity and admiration.

75

'Come out the boy that made that smell,' said Beaker Parker. No-one moved. Pursed lips all round as the boys tried to suppress their giggles. I looked towards my mate Joe as he looked back at me. His pursed lips and goldfish bulging cheeks threatened to explode with merriment and his eyes were saucer-wide with incredulity as Beaker continued.

'Right, all stand and bend over your desks. I will find the culprit.'

The silly sod then began to sniff each boy's backside. This was just too much for me; it was burst or laugh; a great guffaw exploded on the silent class.

Beaker Parker, fairly leapt to my side and grabbed my left ear. My ears were huge compared to my small, narrow head and the boys had nicknamed me Dumbo in recognition of my wonderful flappers. Not for the first time, Beaker attempted to lift me bodily by my ear to the front of the class.

'So you think it's funny, Freeman, eh? Let's see you laugh after this lot!' He grabbed up his cane, thrust me over a front row desk, and attacked my rear end with six mighty blows. Gritting my teeth with pain, I was made to stand on a chair facing my classmates. Trying my hardest not to cry, a tear ran down my face as the pain turned to heat.

The phantom farter was forgotten.

It was no wonder the skin cracked where my ears joined my head. Weeping sores were treated for years in the sickbay. No-one ever asked what caused the problem as Beaker Parker continued regularly to assault my flappers.

My greatest pleasure was sport to which, in its wisdom, the school devoted a lot of time. Especially to running, football and boxing.

All the boys had to take boxing lessons for the first year, and were fortunate to be coached by C.S.M "Dusty" Miller—ex-Army champion. Dusty looked very much a fighter, with his flattened nose and rubbery face. I didn't fancy boxing at all but Dusty treated the boys well and always made us laugh. This approach brought out the best in me and within a year I was selected for the junior boxing team.

The other great love of my life became music, my trade. Two sessions of band practice were held every weekday—an hour before lunch and an hour after the evening meal. For the first three months of band practice the two other newchies and I had only mouthpieces to blow. The school was short of instruments although there were twenty-eight cornet players in all.

A number of bands were picked from all musicians. Marching bands of sixty plus and touring bands, as well as church band for Sundays.

After the initial disappointment of not getting an instrument we had great fun blowing on our mouthpieces. They served a good purpose, hardening the lips whilst we learnt to read music. The cornet players progressed from fourth cornet—umpahs only—to third cornet—to second cornet and counter melody—to first cornet. There were also three soloists. It was my ambition to become a soloist but after five years I only managed to reach first cornet player—and there were eight of them.

With so much to do, the days were filled with activity and interest and the time raced by. My best friend was Joe Skelley. Joe was a newchie in the same room as me and sharing the same classes. He had a freckled face, protruding front teeth, and totally unruly hair. He was well built and, like me, showed little fear of authority. We were almost inseparable.

Joe was an orphan, who had lost his parents tragically when he was eight. He now had an uncle as his guardian whom he didn't like one little bit.

From the earliest days, our main worries moved from homesickness to bullying and hunger. We were kept so busy and active during the day that homesickness overtook us less and less. Often we were so tired, we fell asleep as one of us was telling our bedtime story to the others. I seemed to be the one asked to tell stories after lights-out, and it was always tales of my life in India, especially about bazaars and my friend Anil that fascinated my room-mates.

There were lots of boys for the bullies to choose from for their entertainment and I wasn't disturbed for some time. Both Joe and Alf had been selected on consecutive nights for Pinder's charade but some boys were never troubled, possibly due to their good physique, or because they had relatives among the older big boys or staff.

As the weeks passed, my confidence returned and I became a bit too cheeky for Pinder's liking. I was a skinny lad with a smallish, long head, sharp-featured face and large, protruding ears.

77

I was—on the face of it—an ideal candidate for the bully boys, except they did not know of my background, my upbringing.

The henchmen arrived again in the middle of the night and I was rudely awakened, but this time I wasn't such a terrified, homesick boy. But I was certainly a frightened boy whose heart was trying to get out of his chest as I said, 'No—I'm not coming.'

A struggle ensued as I was dragged down the corridor by five bigger boys to the big room.

As they dumped me in front of the table they released their grip so I could stand up—no doubt feeling safe in front of the bully boss, Pinder. One of the henchmen made a filthy remark about my mother as I was dumped on the floor. I saw red; my mother was my life and the most precious thing in the world to me. I leapt from the floor and let fly a vicious right at the nearest henchman. The blow missed his face but hit his Adam's apple and he let out a scream. Other boys jumped on me as I was lashing out in all directions.

I wasn't sure how it happened, but I came to, lying in front of the table, blood gushing from a cut forehead. All the boys had disappeared except two; Pinder was one of them.

He was saying it was only a joke, just a game. 'Have a cigarette'—I'd never smoked in my life—'Have a bar of chocolate.'

They tried to stop the bleeding with handkerchiefs. The corridor lookout—two of which were always stationed either end of the corridor—came running—'Duty C.S.M coming.' I was hurriedly whisked off to bed.

Questioned the following day by C.S.M. Halyard I would only tell him that I had cut my head on the bunk bed. Whether the C.S.M. suspected foul play is unknown.

I was sent to the surgery to have my cuts treated by Matron and I met C.S.M. Halyard's wife for the first time. Two things came out of this nightmare: Pinder's attitude changed towards me—but I didn't change my feelings for him—and C.S.M. Halyard and his wife seemed to take a special interest in this skinny little boy and his friend Joe who were occasionally invited out for Sunday tea at the Halyards' bungalow in Braunton.

It would be in the fifth or sixth month of my arrival at Saunton when the cut head incident occurred. I had no real thought of protecting Pinder when I lied to my friendly C.S.M., it just seemed the thing to do. I was embarrassed, even ashamed of being dragged down corridors and abused by Pinder and his mates. It was bad enough to have had to endure it without having to admit weakness and fear. Anyway the C.S.M. might not have believed me for I was sure no-one would back me up. Pinder had everyone scared.

At lunchtime the following day a strange thing occurred. The servers returned the dirty main course plates to the servery and came back with steaming rolls of "spotted dick." Large slices swimming in custard were carefully passed, hand to hand, up the table. Eventually wafer thin slices with a dab of custard arrived for me and those in the middle of the table. I glared up the table and met Pinder's eyes. For a moment our eyes locked.

He beckoned the server and murmured in his ear. All eyes watched the server return to the bottom of the table, cut off another slice of spotted dick and carry it up to place on my plate. I looked up the table at Pinder, he smiled down at me.

'Eat it up boy,' he said.

At that moment I hated him more than ever. I lifted the extra slice slowly from the little custard I had and deliberately placed it in the centre of the table. I looked at the fear and amazement on the faces around me. I glanced at Pinder who had gone bright red.

'You'll pay for this boy,' he scowled.

I picked up my spoon and started to eat my wafer thin slice trying my hardest to stop my hand from trembling. I kept repeating under my breath, 'I'm not frightened of you anymore—I'm not frightened of you,' but I was.

Saturday afternoon was the best time of the whole week. We were free to do what we liked, but forbidden to use the local bus that plied its trade between Braunton village and Croyde Bay, passing Saunton every two hours.

Joe and I would leave the hotel at two o'clock and walk the lanes to Braunton, there to gaze in the shop windows and, if we had any money, buy some chips or broken biscuits. Hunger was always with us, and we had endless discussion on how to get more to eat. Parents or guardians were allowed to send a postal order for one shilling and sixpence to the House C.S.M. every fortnight, if they could afford it. Ninepence was saved by the school bank towards the war effort and credited to the boys' account. The other ninepence could be drawn out from the C.S.M. on Saturday mornings at ten o'clock, usually at fourpence halfpenny a time.

Mother did her best, but sometimes a month went by without letter or postal order.

'We ought to be getting back,' said Joe as we passed a shop with a clock in the window.

'Yes,' I replied. 'We've only three quarters of an hour to roll call.'

We made haste along the lanes and through a farm.

'What's that stuff?' I asked, but Joe didn't know.

Passing the edge of the field, I grasped a handful of dark green leaves and pulled, and a white, bulbous object with purplish collar came clean out of the soil.

'Let's take it with us and see what it tastes like,' I said and so began something that was to sustain me and my friends for nearly five years.

That evening, having acquired a knife from someone else's table my room-mates and I sat chewing great slices of swede.

'Good ain't it?' said Alf the Cockney. I smiled; somehow they saw me as leader and I was experiencing comradeship for the first time and a new kind of belonging.

It wasn't long before two floorboards had been loosened under my bunk bed and the cavity below was filled with stolen swede and apples. As the months went by, boys from other rooms appeared at night and pleaded for a slice of this or that. Joe and I took risks in stocking our larder and therefore felt it necessary to make a small charge to boys from other rooms. One halfpenny gave you a choice of anything in the larder. If you couldn't pay you could have tick up to a limit of sixpence.

As the months rolled by and money came in, the shop expanded its range. A tin of unsweetened cocoa was miraculously purchased in Braunton on Saturday for tenpence. Mixed with powdered glue and water, small chocolate balls were dried on the radiators. Fifty-two balls at a penny each—over five hundred per cent profit. This must have been the start of the drug trade, but life was getting better all the time.

I enjoyed the daily square-bashing, but one or two of my mates had missed out when God had handed out co-ordination. Left got mixed up with right, and some of the drill commands saw the squad going in two different directions at once.

We learnt the intricate art of forming fours on the march and changing from quick time to slow time. Joe and I could always see the funny side of the mistakes that were made and we would be sent running continuously round the parade ground as punishment while our mates did the drill.

The school supported the war effort (and local community fund-raising) in every possible way. Salute the Soldier Week was a national event and the Dukies did their bit.

On one such occasion, the marching band, including third cornet player Bob Freeman, was in a procession through the centre of Barnstaple. It was a fine day in late summer and crowds lined the streets. The procession had completed the outward march, and was to return after a fifteen minute halt.

The bandmaster stood the band down saying, 'Take a rest, boys—don't sit on the grass—and don't roam away.'

I had been watching the crowd as we marched through the streets playing, and had spotted an ice cream parlour just a street away. 'I'll just nip across and get a couple of ices,' I said.

Joe who was a fourth cornet player by now, pleaded with me not to go in case my absence was noticed. I would have none of it and took off, well out of sight of the bandmaster.

The ice cream parlour wasn't in the next street as I had thought but I eventually found it and purchased two three halfpenny cornets. Holding my instrument in one hand and two ice creams in the other, I hurried back only to hear the band strike up "Imperial Echoes."

Rounding the final corner I saw the band disappearing in the distance and my heart sank. Panic set in. One or two of the crowd had noticed me and put two and two together; some laughter, more pity. I stood there in panic.

'I know the route they're taking, son—come with me.'

This marvellous grey-haired old gent—probably a first world war soldier—quickly manoeuvred me through a few back streets and reached the main road.

'Right, son—stand behind me and don't move. As they pass, and when we get up to the cornet players, I'll give you the signal.'

I stood in the crowd, crouching low, as the band came marching up. At the signal, I darted down the column of cornet players, almost tripping myself and a colleague up in the process. The ice creams went flying. There was a cheer from the crowd as I darted in, but the bandmaster and drum major were unaware of what was happening behind them. I hadn't been missed and no-one in authority was the wiser, but these escapades were building up a reputation for me amongst the boys which could backfire. Poor Joe didn't get his ice cream and I wished that I could have thanked the knowing, grey-haired gent who had saved my bacon.

The band toured many southern towns during the war years and the boys always hoped that they would be picked to go on the trip. Not only was it exciting to perform in public but one could almost guarantee a slap-up meal afterwards, irrespective of rationing.

As well as marching bands, I was also chosen to play at evening concerts in various towns. This required different music again; I took great interest and delight in these occasions and tried very hard at practice sessions.

The height of my musical career came out of the blue in 1943. A small number of the band were to have a half of an evening's programme in Ilfracombe.

I had just been promoted to first cornet player and was sitting on the stage before the curtain went up when one of the soloists was suddenly attacked with acute stomach pains.

'Freeman,' said the bandmaster. 'Change places with Humphries and take his part in the "Two Finches".' I was terrified.

The "Two Finches" was a cornet duo and the *piece de resistance* of the night's programme. Such was the marvellous training given to the boys that the duo went off without a hitch and, to rapturous applause from the audience, my colleague and I stood up and bowed. All the practice sessions—which had included playing solos—had paid dividends, and it was at times such as this that I thought of my Mother. I only wished she could have seen me.

11

THE YANKS HAD ARRIVED. In 1943 an American army unit set up a tented village on the sand dunes below the cliffs. At morning assembly in the ballroom the R.S.M. addressed us all in a stern and powerful voice.

'You will no longer be allowed on the beach or sand dunes unless it's in a planned, authorised and accompanied swimming party.'

Our swimming pool was the sea, and up to now we had been at liberty to traverse the beach and dunes which both Joe, Alf and I had done regularly, scavenging for anything we could find. The schoolmasters took us for a swim once a week in the summer.

The R.S.M. continued, 'The American camp is out of bounds and the sand dunes will be mined. Minefields—you know what that means? It means death. Barbed wire and notices will be placed round all minefields. Any boy caught below the cliffs will be disciplined.'

He put the fear of God into us that day . . . and also not a little excitement. Americans at Saunton. Nothing much had happened for two years. We wondered what difference it would make.

Our first contact with the Yanks was through boxing.

Dusty gathered us together in the gymnasium to give us the good news.

'You will be pleased to know the Commandant has agreed that the boxing team will stage an exhibition for the American Army.' Cheers and excited chatter erupted in the gymnasium.

'Quiet a minute, quiet—we have a week to prepare and you will be fighting the same partners as last week's exhibition. Now get on with your training and let me see you work hard.'

The boxing team had put on exhibitions before in many local town halls for various War Effort events. We never fought opponents from other schools but always Dukie versus Dukie.

What the public didn't realise was the same two boys fought each other time and again.

A bout was only three rounds of three minutes each, red sash versus blue sash. I had thirty-one public fights in my five years, twenty-seven of them against the same opponent. I won only five times in all my matches.

My main opponent was an Irish boy called Shaun Daughton who was a good friend out of the ring and as neither of us had much of a punch there was never a knock-out.

Dusty trained his boys well. He would slowly trace the target area to score points with his finger, talking all the time.

'The target area is a line running over the centre of the head, behind the ears, down the neck, behind the arms and down to the waist. Clench your fists correctly—thumb on the outside or you'll break it—no points for slapping. Always keep one foot forward, the other to the rear. Balance is most important. Keep on your toes. Left jab, left jab, left jab—if you get a clear shot at the chin throw your right,' and so it went on. Dusty was patient and many boys went on to become army champions.

Dusty's gymnasium was the converted underground car park. As well as a boxing ring, there were punch bags, exercise mats, medicine balls, skipping ropes, wall bars, and a wooden horse. The gym was open most nights of the week and Dusty was always around to encourage the keenest.

The team was picked and Shaun and I joined the party. We were marched from the school down to the tented village and I made a special note of the route we took through the barbed wire across the sand dunes.

A talkative GI and Dusty Miller led the column of boys through the camp entrance. We negotiated rows of small tents and guy-ropes. A very large marquee took up the centre of the camp. Grinning faces of GI's appeared at tent doorways shouting encouragement and joking. Others strolled towards the marquee.

'Daughton! Freeman!—Are you with us?' called out Dusty.

'Here, sir,' we chorused.

'Good, because you two are on first. You have thirty minutes to get changed. All of you change in this small tent. I'll be back shortly. Don't leave the tent.'

Dusty returned five minutes later looking rather concerned.

'Gather round lads. Quiet now—I've looked at the ring that the Americans have rigged up and it's small and higher off the ground than you're used to, so be prepared. There are two other things you'll find different from our previous exhibitions. One, the noise. The Americans will be shouting out encouragement but you must concentrate on your boxing skills. Secondly, the marquee is already hazy with cigar smoke so be prepared. Remember, we are here to entertain, to show off our skills—so get to it and let's have a good show.'

Fully gloved up, we entered the huge marquee to a babble of noisy whoops and cheers. A makeshift boxing ring had been erected in the centre of the tent and GI's were seated on all four sides, with some standing at the back. The first two rows of seats were occupied by V.I.P.s with a few wives amongst them. I noticed C.S.M. Halyard near the front, with his wife.

The boxers split into two groups. Red sashes on one side of the ring—blue sashes on the other. I always wanted to pee before a fight and was thankful that I was first on that night.

Announcements were being made by the M.C. who was making quite a long job of it—no doubt trying to impress both British and Americans on this, our first get-together.

At last I was in the ring, the gong sounded, gloves touched and away we went, showing the splendid techniques of well-trained boxers, taught to box by scoring points.

No doubt the Americans were used to brawlers, big punchers providing plenty of action and so they must have been somewhat surprised at the sight of two skinny boys prancing about, flicking out left jabs and retreating. Nevertheless they seemed to be enjoying the spectacle if the noise was anything to go by. Whoops, hollers and advice rained in from all quarters and this was a totally new experience for the boxers. Normally, with a British audience, amateur boxing was watched and appreciated in almost silence.

'Go on, kid—send him to Popsi!' The noise was horrendous.

Round two began. The ring seemed much smaller than Dusty's and the ropes were thinner and slack. The floor was a tarpaulin sheet spread over long planks raised three feet from the ground upon trestles, and Shaun and I bounced around on the springy surface like ping-pong balls. Lightweight as we were, the planks nevertheless vibrated alarmingly with every attacking flurry. Shaun was boxing differently, he seemed to have lost his rhythm. The noise was ear-splitting.

Round three, and the noise, and/or the encouragement, seemed to affect Shaun. He was more aggressive than he had ever been before and was attacking with flurries of lefts and rights; I couldn't understand what had got into him. Sod you, I thought, trying to show off to the Americans. So I began to mix it.

The encouragement grew even greater as we stood, toe to toe, swinging wildly at each other. So engrossed were we in the novel departure from our normally sedate routine we were unaware that the trestles below the tarpaulin had started to drift apart. The floor of the ring began to sink in the middle and Shaun and I slowly disappeared from sight, flaying the life out of each other as we did so. The Yanks cheered, whistled and laughed as we vanished from view. No doubt all present that evening will have recounted this story many times over.

After being left alone by Pinder and his gang for some time, I was again dragged from my bunk late one night and manhandled up the corridor. There sat fat Pinder, stern faced behind his blanketed table . . . but not so frightening now that I knew what to expect. Four bigger boys held onto me firmly as I struggled to get free. I glared hatred at Pinder.

'Right, boy—I brought you here to warn you, so listen care—'

'Don't call me boy, Pinder, you know my—'

Pinder leapt to his feet and slapped me hard across the face with his open hand. My cheek flamed with the ferocity of the blow.

'Shut up!' he screamed. 'Shut up and listen. *I'm* the one that will be chosen for the vacant position of Solo Cornet Player or your life won't be worth living. Hear me, boy. You'd better make a mess of your solo on the try-out or else.'

'I'm better than you Pinder—and you know it, even if you have been playing longer. I will win—you'll see,' I said, struggling to get free.

Pinder leant back in his chair with an evil smile on his face.

'I know about your food store. I've just been biding my time. If you want to keep it, with my help—you'd better lose that audition—d'ya understand, you little bastard?'

'Never, and you're the bastard.'

Pinder flashed to his feet again sending his chair scuttling. Again he swung at me. I saw the blow coming and jerked back out of range. My minders were off balance as I came free and threw a punch at the evil face in front of me.

A shrill whistle froze everyone in the room. The duty C.S.M. holding the look-out by the scruff of the neck surveyed the scene.

In boxing kit, Pinder and I stood shivering inside the ropes of the boxing ring. The gymnasium was full of boys standing in rows, shortest at the front. Dusty Miller was sitting at the side of the ring by a small table with a brass bell on it. He held a stop watch in his hand. The audience was silent.

The R.S.M. stood on the side of the boxing ring, glaring at the sea of faces.

'These two boys were caught fighting after lights-out. Fighting is an offence that will not go unpunished. Both boys have had one month's privileges withdrawn and are confined to the school building.   Fighting is for the boxing ring and nowhere else, remember that. I hope they both get a good hiding. Carry on, sergeant.'

Dusty climbed into the ring as the buzz of excited conversation filled the gym.

'You're not one of my boxers Pinder so I'll warn you now. No hitting below the belt. Keep your gloves clenched and fight fairly. Now get to your corners.'

From the bell Pinder charged, I wasn't expecting it and got clobbered by a flurry of windmill punches. I was knocked to the floor. The noise of the shouting and screaming audience made it impossible to hear the count. I rose to my feet as Dusty, with one hand on each side of my face, looked into my eyes.

'Are you okay, Freeman?'

'Yes, sir.'

'Well keep moving and remember your footwork.'

He stood back and shouted, 'Box on!'

For three hectic rounds we hammered one another. Both of us were well bloodied and still flaying each other as the last bell sounded and we were dragged apart. Dusty simultaneously raised a gloved hand of each boxer as the R.S.M. looked on. I grinned at Pinder—Pinder glared back. The noisy boys cheered, but why, I never quite understood. A week later I failed my audition for the solo cornet vacancy—so did Pinder. The place went to a quiet boy who was one of only two cornet players who possessed his own instrument, bought by his loving mother as a birthday present. I now had two reasons to be envious of him.

Life followed a fairly regular pattern, day in, day out. I rarely thought of my family now. Our days were so full of preparing for band outings, boxing exhibitions or annual exams. My schooling was improving and I was achieving reasonable results, especially in Military History, Maths and Map Reading, but my main interests were firmly centred on my Bflat cornet and my boxing skills.

As Joe, Alf and I left the newchie category and became fully fledged Dukies we became braver and more daring. Saturday came round again in that summer of 1943 and I well remember walking out the entrance of the school with another hundred or so noisy boys. The afternoon was ours and most of the boys were making for the village of Braunton to spend their few pennies. My friend Joe was playing football for the school team so Alf and I were at a loose end.

'Shall we go down the village?' asked Alf.

'No—everybody's going there,' I said.

'Well let's go and watch Joe then.'

'I've got a better idea,' I said. Let's get over this wall and I'll tell you.'

We climbed a drystone wall opposite the school entrance on the far side of the B road that ran round to Croyde Bay, and squatted down on our haunches.

'Well—what is it?' asked Alf.

I took a deep breath and paused, looking at Alf. He stared back at me wondering why I looked so excited.

'Well?' he said.

'Visit the Yanks,' I burst out grinning.

'You're crackers! Out of bounds and minefields. You're joking.'

I eased my back against the sharp flints in the wall.

'No—it will be easy. I've been thinking of it for ages. I made a special note of the way Dusty took us through the barbed wire when we went boxing. It's easy—I'll show you.'

'What if we get caught. You know what . . . '

'No chance. Dusty's duty C.S.M. and he won't leave the school building. There's no-one else about. Come on, you'll love the Yanks.'

Reluctantly Alf followed and off we went.

The ground before us rose fairly steeply into grassy fields, and Alf and I set off for the summit. Once over the crest of the hill we made a detour back toward Braunton for half a mile and then dropped down the hill, over a road, and were soon on the edge of the sand dunes, in line with the American camp. Within minutes we were picking our way between guy ropes and tents. There had been no-one in the sentry box by the barbed wire flanking the main entrance, but that was probably logical, because the Germans wouldn't invade at two-thirty on a Saturday afternoon, and obviously the Americans knew this.

'Hey, buddy—are you soldier boys from up there?' said a loud voice.

We jumped with surprise as no-one seemed to be in sight. A big smiling and chewing face appeared in the doorway of a tent behind us.

'Hey, Jed, Hank—lookee what I've got here.'

Very soon a crowd of American soldiers surrounded us.

'What's that number on your hat for, kid?' asked a guy in a vest and shorts.

'That's my number—M34,' I said. 'I'm in Marlborough House.'

'Are you real soldiers? Can you fire a gun?' he said laughing.

'Sure,' I said, gaining confidence all the time.

'Let's see you march then, kid,' said Fatso.

Alf and I, confident and showing off, proceeded to march in twos—I was giving the orders.

'Quick march—left, right, left, right,' I called out the time. 'About turn. Left, right, left, forward. Changing to slow time—slow-o-march,' and we performed like two tin robots.

The Americans were impressed and we found ourselves being treated to cookies and coffee. We left the camp some ten minutes later, pockets stuffed with cookies, chewing gum and a packet of Camel cigarettes. I had the Americans to thank for starting me smoking, although most of the Camels were sold in our secret shop, and smoked on the balcony late at night. This was the first of half a dozen visits which we managed to get away with over the next eighteen months.

The week following my first visit to the Yanks I received a letter. Mother used to write occasionally and this was the only news I had of the outside world. All foodstuffs were now on ration, she said, and I worried myself sick with the news. I imagined Mother, brothers and sister Pauline dying of hunger. Mum found it hard to manage at the beginning of the war, so how could she possibly manage now?

She wrote that they had moved again. They were now living at number four, Britannia Road, Warley, Brentwood, Essex, an army married quarter at last, now the damage had been done, now I'd lost my two brothers.

Mum had long recovered from her illness and Vic had returned home from one of Dad's brothers to the family fold, so they were all together, except Father. He was now a tank instructor and was stationed at the Fighting Vehicle Proving Establishment (F.V.P.E.) at Chertsey, Surrey. According to Mum's letter Dad only got home every three or four weeks. Poor old Mum—still shouldering the burden of bringing up the family.

It was after this letter that we received the most exciting news that I'd ever had in my life.

We were at our normal morning assembly. Prayers had been said and the usual day was in prospect, but then the R.S.M. took the podium. Whenever the R.S.M. took the podium we stood up straighter, braced ourselves for more orders or instructions, or more often than not heard of misdemeanours or punishments. We waited on his words.

'Pay attention,' he barked. A muted conversation started up.

'All boys who have a home to go to, and provided that home is NOT in London, will get six weeks home leave in July and August. Next of kin will be contacted and arrangements made. Those . . . quiet, no talking!' he barked as excited conversation filled the room. The room went silent again.

'Those boys without a home to go to will go to farms. More information will be given to you by your Company Sergeant Majors in the next two weeks.'

The assembly hall erupted in excited conversation as the R.S.M. stepped down off the podium.

I just couldn't believe it—it was over two years since I had seen my mother. Father had visited me once, but could only stay for a few hours. The prospect of seeing my mother and the family again seemed unbelievable. The whole world seemed to change, and memories of that part of my life that had been virtually blanked out—buried for more than two years—now came flooding back.

Mum, Vic, Ernie and Pauline all waiting for me to come home; it seemed like a dream.

12

WE MARCHED TO THE STATION SINGING all the way. Was there ever such a happy crowd of boys? A special train had been arranged to take us directly to Waterloo. Our families were to meet us off the train.

Before embarking we were each issued with a gas mask in a cardboard box on string straps, plus a box full of sandwiches. Each of us had a label on a loop of string hung round his neck.

'Keep these labels on until your parents take them off,' the R.S.M. commanded as he issued his final instructions before we boarded the train.

I read my label: 'Robert Freeman, Liverpool Street Station to Brentwood,' it proclaimed.

Once the train got moving, most of the boys, myself included, removed the stupid labels and began the fun and games only a trainload of deliriously happy boys could invent. Away from authority, we let rip with every daft game and every rude song we could muster. If Hitler had seen three hundred grinning boys in steamed-up gas masks, leaning out of carriage windows and cavorting up and down the corridors, he would have surrendered right away. Fortunately no accidents occurred, and after an hour or so things settled down to one of anticipation and excitement as we impatiently waited to meet our loved ones.

The train slowed down and then crawled through the outskirts of London with all boys standing impatiently, dying for it to get to the station. Before the train came to a halt, the first in the queue had risked their limbs by jumping off to find their parents. Soon everybody was on the platform either looking for a special familiar face or being embraced by a loving family. I couldn't see Father anywhere. The majority of boys were found by their families or vice versa and the crowd thinned out. Still no Father to be seen. I became nervous and eventually stood there totally alone not knowing what to do. A porter noticed the little boy in uniform and asked what was wrong.

'My Dad's not here,' I said tearfully.

'Don't fret, son. He's probably been delayed. Come with me and we will soon find your Dad.'

I was taken to the stationmaster's office and given a mug of tea and a cake. An announcement was made on the loudspeaker but no Father appeared. I was questioned as to where I was going.

I had long since lost my label. My last home had been in Worcester. This was my first time in London. In my frightened state I could only think of one word from the card that had been hung round my neck and that word was 'Liverpool.'

'Ah,' said the stationmaster. 'that's where your father will be,' and he made arrangements for me to be escorted to Euston Station and put on the Liverpool train with the guard.

I sat in the guard's van and was happy to be on my way home—or so I thought. Arriving at Lime Street Station late at night I was handed over to the stationmaster. He had no knowledge of my father and everyone was at a loss what to do. I was given a seat by a blazing coal fire in the stationmaster's office and was offered a meal. The police were called and searched my pockets, coming up with a temporary six-week ration book and details of the Dukies' School. I slept fitfully that night in the porters' cabin, and they looked after me well, intrigued by the little boy soldier.

What Mother was going through can only be surmised, but the police soon solved the mystery and I was dispatched back to Euston and successfully met there by Father. The family reunion at Britannia Road was one of tearful happiness. As I walked into the living room of the strange house Mother looked up from the kitchen sink, arms deep in suds. Hands dripping, she rushed forward and clutched me to her, tears welling up in her eyes.

'Oh, Bobby,' she cried. 'You're so big and how smart you look in your uniform; how are you, darling?' She crushed the breath out of me with her hugging and kissing. 'Fred, just look at him, hasn't he grown, doesn't he look well? A bit thin though—oh, it's lovely to have you home!' And the adoration continued.

I found this all strange and embarrassing. I wasn't used to close bodily contact and being kissed. It was over two years since I'd seen them all and I'd got used to my own world, my lonely world; I didn't depend on anybody.

That night as I lay in my bed I overheard Mum and Dad talking.

'He's changed, Vi, so don't smother him, give him time; who knows what he's gone through these last few years.'

Why Dad hadn't turned up at Waterloo was never mentioned and the next day he had to return to his unit. I was happy to be with the family again. Vic looked much bigger and broader than I remembered. At thirteen years he looked really grown up although I had shot up over a foot, according to Mother, and was equally as tall as Vic. Ernie and Pauline were babies no longer and Pauline was quite a little lady at five years old.

It soon became apparent that the life-style I'd known so well at Worcester hadn't changed. Mum now drew her army allowance on Fridays from Warley Post Office. As it was the school holidays we all went with her. From the post office we walked the half mile back down towards Warley Hill where there was a café, and we were treated to sausage and mash.

Each family had ration books and these books were registered at certain grocers. Mum would then go into Brentwood and do the bulk of her week's shopping. We three boys would go home; Pauline went with Mother.

It wasn't long before I realised the same pattern of hand-to-mouth existence continued as previously. The family ate well until Tuesday and then things got short. There was not even cooking fat to fry with so we used a bit of margarine until that, too, had gone. There was no sugar; only saccharin. No real eggs—but I did love the powdered variety. There was no shortage of ration coupons—just money.

To raise cash Mum was now using "Uncle's," the pawn shop. Anything that would fetch a shilling was hocked. I well remember going with Mum when she hocked a tennis racquet and racquet press. Some time later when Dad came home, he searched the house high and low for them.

'Vi,' he said, 'have you seen that racquet of mine?'

'Try the attic,' said Vi. I was sworn to secrecy and Dad never cottoned on.

I was a novelty those first few days and although I discarded my uniform as soon as I got home, Mother persuaded me, on every possible occasion, to put it on so that she could show me off to all her friends and neighbours. Whenever we went uptown or anywhere out of the street it was 'Bobby, be a good boy, put your uniform on—just for me,' and I was shown off to everyone she met.

Our home at Britannia Road was number four in a terrace of twenty houses. It had a small garden in front of an entrance porch, a narrow hall with two doors on the left, one into the front room and the other into a living room. To the right were open stairs rising to a narrow landing from which three bedrooms opened off, together with, (a new experience for me), a bathroom with an enamel tub on four legs.

The living room was about fourteen feet square and the wall facing its door was almost totally occupied by a black cast iron range, combining a fireplace and large oven. There was a mantlepiece above the range and alcoves both sides. The room's righthand wall had a sash window which looked out over a concreted yard, containing a mangle with wooden rollers and an outside toilet. Beyond was a sixty foot garden. A door from the living room led into a narrow kitchen which was painted in brown gloss up to four feet from the floor and dark green gloss from thence to the ceiling. Someone, probably Dad, had attempted to paint an inch wide black line between the green and the brown, but had failed to make it a straight one.

A gas cooker, copper clothes boiler, enamel sink and wooden draining-board completed the furnishings of the kitchen, which had a total of four doors. One opened on to the outside yard, one led to the living room, one to a small walk-in pantry, and the fourth door, fitted under the stairs, led to the coal hole.

By the end of the first week in my strange new home I was really enjoying the cushy life. One evening the family were seated round the faithful kitchen table—Vic, Pauline, Ernie and I—admiring the mountain of bread and marge that took pole position in the centre of the red and white check oilcloth. Mum was doing us a treat before we went to bed. This was an extra; we didn't usually have supper, but Mum had managed to get some frying fat from the British Restaurant where she worked and we had been promised our favourite food, chips.

'Don't touch that bread or you won't get any chips,' said Mum to us all, but really to Vic.

We kept looking through the connecting door to the kitchen, breathing our favourite perfume of hot fat and watching Mother trying to turn the million chips that filled a large army issue frying pan to the brim. The bubbling fat was spitting higher and higher

94

up the wall, gas blazed at full blast as usual, as we impatiently and excitedly awaited our treat. The black-out curtains were drawn and the single bulb in its coolie hat army shade threw light over the table but left the corners and sides of the room dark.

Mother was no disciplinarian and we always stayed up late. Only when Father was home did we have to go to bed at set times, depending on age. It was a double treat really, because Mum had also acquired a bottle of brown sauce, a rare treat, which Vic had made sure was nearest to him. Still, I thought, he can't use it all, it's a new bottle. Chip sandwiches and brown sauce: was there ever a better meal?

Mum came in with the lovely hot chips and doled them out on to the plates in front of us. We were all watching each other's plates, jealous and envious, doing quick counts, but Mum was faster. Her fingers plucked a chip or two from one plate and put it on another to cause a frown or a smile, ignoring protests. The race was on. Vic, as usual, was first away.

'Don't be greedy, Victor; put some of that back, said Mum, as he cleared the top of the mountain of bread and christened it with half a bottle sauce. No stopping him now, I thought, as he piled his chips onto the bread, slapped another lump of bread on top of the chips and had a sandwich two inches deep. He'll never get his mouth round that, I thought, but, by God, he did, grease, marge and brown sauce running halfway round his great beaming face.

A siren was wailing; I'd never heard one before; it was quite weird and frightening.

'Sod it,' said Mother, who was prone to use a few soft swear words from time to time. 'Another air raid; come on, let's go down the shelter.'

'I'm staying here,' said Vic. 'It's a waste of time going down that place; it's smelly and wet too.'

'You'll come with us or I'll tell your father when he gets home.'

'Oh, Mum,' Vic whined.

We got up from the table, carrying our precious chip butties. Mother returned from upstairs with some blankets.

'Take these,' she said to Vic, 'and switch the light off before we open the door.'

The siren was now competing with Pauline's cries. Nobody seemed to realize that this was all strange to me; there was so much for Mum to think about, I suppose. With Pauline in her arms and Ernie holding her hand, I followed them down the two back kitchen steps and up the sixty foot muddy garden.

It was a dismal summer's night as we tramped along and I noticed most backdoors, some with lights still burning, spewing out bodies as mothers shepherded their flocks towards the safe haven of the communal air raid shelter which was on a piece of land at the back of the gardens.

The shelter was made of corrugated, curved steel and covered with earth. We went down eight concrete steps. Wooden slat benches ran along both sides of the narrow space. The floor was covered in stagnant water and bricks and wood had been laid as stepping stones. There were two entrances, one at either end and families were entering from both.

We clambered on to the damp slatted benches, knees under chins and someone lit a candle. It was cold and a baby was crying its head off. All us children sat talking, occasionally breaking off when we heard a loud explosion in the distance, but the mothers seemed to take the raid in their stride. They just chatted to each other as if nothing was happening. After three years of war and the blitz, air raids had become a way of life to them, but not to me. I huddled in my blanket seemingly the only person seriously scared as I listened for aero engines and the occasional explosions outside.

It seemed that the German planes regularly off-loaded their bombs some distance short of their London targets if they encountered night fighters, or even the threat of them. This was a dangerous area to live in and I did see on my second leave a year later a crashed German bomber not four hundred yards from the shelter. Later still on further home leaves, after several shelters had received direct hits, members of the family preferred to sit under the kitchen table and take their chances.

Nobody ever mentioned John or Graham now. Outwardly Mum appeared to have fully recovered, but there must have been times when the memories returned, sparked off by a photograph, a tune, or just a neighbour's kid called John. Who knows what inner scars were left, and in Mum's quieter reflective moments she must have cried for the three children she had lost.

We, the four survivors, benefited from the abundant love and care that she showered on us.

Lying in my single bed, with Ernie in his single bed, in our shared bedroom on my first few nights of leave, I heard Mother singing. She was singing to baby Pauline the same lullaby she had sung to us as children. It was lovely to be back. Listening to Mother would cloak me in warm happiness and security as I drifted off to sleep.

Monday morning was a sight to behold, washing day.

'Vic, Bobby, go upstairs and bring down all the dirty clothes you can find,' said Mum. 'I've got the sheets; look under the beds.'

Down we came with armfuls of woollens, shorts, shirts, towels and dumped them on the cold, stone kitchen floor. The three foot round copper was boiling, throwing clouds of steam into the Turkish bath of a kitchen, water streaming down the gloss painted wall. Mother appeared like an apparition, headscarf tied under her chin, from the direction of the sink.

'Good boys. You're sure there's no more up there? Have you looked in all the bedrooms?'

'Yes, Mum.'

She then sorted the mountain of clothes into different piles. Woollens, sheets, coloureds and the really mucky stuff that needed a good scrub, our shirts, socks and short trousers.

'Where's the scrubbing board?'

'Don't know, Mum.'

'Well, go and look for it—it's not in the kitchen.'

The scrubbing board was an essential part of washing day. One foot wide by two foot long, the face was metal fluted and the board was placed in the sink along with the clothes and hot, steamy soap suds. Jammed between the back of the sink and Mother's stomach, the grubbiest clothes were soaped with the bar of Sunlight soap and then rubbed hard and rapidly up and down the scrubbing board before being thrown into the boiling copper.

It was duly found. Vic had been using it—in anticipation of skiffle.

'Put a handful of Lux flakes in the copper for me, Vic,' said Mum. 'Don't go mad with them—that's all we've got.' Vic always overdid things and grinned his mischievous smile.

Poor Mum was wreathed in sweat, or was it steam? We couldn't see from one end of the kitchen to the other and the floor was already awash.

'Coo-ee, Vi, it's only me.' If I had a pound for every time I'd heard that call I'd be rich, I thought.

Mrs Doe, our next door neighbour, glided through the mist.

'Come in, Jean,' said Mum. 'I was just going to put the kettle on.'

Same old words, not really true but they believed it was.

Any excuse to stop for a natter was always welcome. There never seemed to be any urgency in life. Great friendships were enjoyed by all the wives whom God had cast into the same boat. Back doors were never locked, often never closed. 'Coo-ee, Vi, it's only me,' sounded off daily and very often more than once. Much of life's enjoyment consisted of visits, gossip and a fag. Yes, Mother was smoking cigarettes now. The washing would get done sometime, it always had, and the ironing would get done another day, because that's the way life was.

I soon became familiar with the little general store that played such a big part in the lives of the locals. The old fashioned shop was run by a spinster. Mother had a slate going and paid a little off her mounting debt from time to time to keep the old girl happy. Many a time Vic or I were sent out late at night to knock on the side door of the shop because we were short of some essential foodstuff.

Armed with coupons or points, but no money, we would say, 'Please, Miss Outrem, could Mum have some tea?' The old girl was obliging most of the time but always reminded us to tell Mum what shop hours were. When the spinster occasionally refused us we were sent to neighbours for half a loaf of bread or a cup of sugar or flour—'Mum said she will give you it back as soon as she gets her rations'—same story every time.

Looking back, it is an amazing paradox of life that without question the have nots would always help their own kind. All families in the street were basically in the same position but shared what they had with their neighbours; poverty was pooled. Great happiness was enjoyed by many of these families, for happiness was in the heart and spirit—not in material possessions. Not once can I recall being refused a half cup of sugar or flour. How different from the Lady of the Manor at Suckley in Worcestershire, but of course she had been a have, not a have not.

All these experiences were new to me, as was the tallyman. He called weekly. Mum was a soft touch to sell anything to, especially if it was for her children.

'Only another shilling a week, Mrs Freeman,' and Mum was hooked.

Mum knew the time of day he would call for his weekly payment and he could be spotted through the front room lace curtains calling at neighbours. Two different techniques were employed when Mum hadn't the money to pay her week's dues.

Vic would be told to answer the door—while everyone else hid in the back room—and say, 'Sorry, me Mum's gone out.'

The unbelieving tallyman would ask, 'Did she leave the money?'

'No.'

'When will she be back?'

'Don't know.'

'Tell her I've been and will call back.'

Or alternatively we all hid in the back room with Mum holding a finger to her lips as the tallyman knocked hell out of the front door. The crafty beggar, desperate to catch up on our arrears sometimes came round to the back door. We could spot him early thanks to a sixty foot garden. It was then all change and scramble upstairs, the children giggling and Mum trying to hush us up.

During my third week Dad came home for some leave and now all the family were together for the first time in years. Dad had mellowed a lot and was very caring to us all. He had managed somehow to obtain a few extras from the cookhouse, a large tin of cooking fat, some tins of corned beef, bully biscuits and cheese. He even brought a dozen fresh herrings wrapped in newspaper.

That evening the whole family sat round a blazing fire in the big, black grate of the living room; fortunately it was baking day so the fire was lit. The radio was on in the right-hand alcove.

The walls were covered with pictures. We always had masses of pictures hanging on the walls, all family photographs. Mum and Dad's wedding picture hung over the mantlepiece. There was a photograph of Dad on his horse in full uniform, shiny helmet and lance, his mother and father and many more.

The living room was the most used room in the house. As you entered it from the hallway your eyes fell first on six brass egg cups on a small brass tray, a brass cigarette and matchbox set, Mum's knitting, a sad dusty flower vase feeling redundant, a Taj Mahal engraved brass biscuit barrel, a lost saucer full of pins with a candle stub in the middle, all old friends sharing the top of the sideboard that Dad had varnished.

One of the top two drawers of the sideboard was never quite closed; there was always something hanging out its mouth. Stuffed indiscriminately with papers, various broken Christmas bits and pieces, an old apron, half used candles, unwound string, buttons and broken hair clips, and a kitchen knife, all of which came out weekly for an airing when Mother searched for the insurance book, or the tallyman's book. Then they all went back in for another week's rest.

Your eyes then moved to the mantlepiece over the huge black range. A pair of eight inch black china horses stood either end of the shelf, but, most importantly, there stood the clock. This family heirloom took up pole position in the centre of the mantlepiece, directly under Mum and Dad's wedding picture.

Looking back I suppose it was the little inscribed plate that made all the difference.

Presented to Trooper F.C. Freeman
Best kept garden
1934/36

I don't suppose Dad had won much in his life, well you didn't in those days, but to win something as grand as a clock and to have it presented to you by the Commanding Officer while the whole Regiment looked on—well, I ask you—who wouldn't be proud?

Of course all this happened when I was a nipper, I didn't know Dad was good at gardening, not then, so good in fact that he had won the annual competition three years in succession, hence the special presentation of the clock. But, it wasn't just the clock itself which made it important. It was what it represented: the memories and the emotions it evoked. When you're bottom of the pile, just a trooper in a Cavalry regiment, you're not likely to get noticed much, but the whole Regiment had witnessed the presentation, heard his name read out, seen him marching up to the C.O.

Mother used to recount the story to us all and her eyes would shine with pride as she remembered the hushed scene on the parade ground, Dad marching forward, his magnificent bearing and all the envious looks of the other young troopers' wives.

It was easy to imagine how the clock had looked on the day of presentation. The solid body of highly polished mahogany shaped like a domed mountain was mounted on a thick grey base of marble. The two and a half inch dial was centred in the mahogany with two black and gold hands for hours and minutes and a long slim gold second hand. I remember gazing up at that clock many times over the years, it was always in the centre of the mantelpiece over big black grates. Except in hot spicy lands where it enjoyed the luxury of a low coffee table under the ceiling mounted brass fans.

But now it was back in England once again, much aged from its travels. Its coat was now one of black paint, cracked and peeling in places and a corner of the thick marble base had been left behind where the sun shone every day. Back in yet another married quarter it sat forlornly on the high mantelpiece under the picture of my parents, Mum in her beautiful white wedding gown and Dad in his best blues.

On each end of the mantelpiece reared the eight inch china horses with multiple fractures. Between the horses and the clock, dishes of pins and buttons, propped up photographs, tubes of spills, curling tongs, a miniature chalk rabbit, and an overstuffed brass letter holder all fought for space.

The clock showed three twenty-six. It had been three twenty-six when we were last in Risalpur, three twenty-six when we went through the Kyhber Pass to Hell's Kitchen. It was still three twenty-six when we did lifeboat drill and Mum cried because there was no room in the boats for men. And then England and war. After a year travelling around Worcester and surviving the fire, Mum unpacked the clock—and it was still three twenty-six. Never mind, Mum was happy, Dad was home.

We enjoyed the herrings Dad had grilled on the toasting fork, one by one, in front of glowing coals in the old black grate and now Mum cleared the pine-scrubbed table as Tommy Handley's voice answered Mrs Mopp's 'Can I do yer now, sir?'

Father lifted down his battered clock and stared at it deep in thought.

Mother's knitting needles were clicking away robot style as she smiled from one to the other of us.

Father moved his chair back from the fire to the kitchen table. He laid clean newspaper over the pinewood and placed the clock in front of him. 'Fetch me a saucer, Vic, will you?

He then proceeded to dismantle the clock, bit by bit, carefully and methodically, laying every cog, stem, backplate, wheel and spring on clean paper, in sequence, and numbering every item as he went. We watched fascinated at the concentration and care Father was putting into the job. He carefully cleaned each item with a feather dipped in a saucer of petrol, after which he re-assembled the pieces in reverse order and with another feather lightly touched oil on to the moving parts.

He then rewound the clock, gave it a final polish, shook it and placed it centre of the mantelpiece where it ticked loudly for twenty-one excited seconds and then rested.

'Bugger it,' said Dad.

The clock showed three twenty-seven—it had advanced a minute in five years.

Dad was good at amusing us all; Monopoly was a whole family affair and many happy evenings were spent round the kitchen table involved in this and many other games.

I seemed to be totally accepted now and in fact Mother, embarrassingly for me, seemed to be favouring me more than the others. Perhaps it was my absence, perhaps my skinny, neglected appearance, perhaps my imagination, for I wasn't used to being loved and cared for.

The days flew by. Dad treated us elder boys once or twice to the pictures and swimming baths. On the Sunday of Dad's leave we all went out for a picnic and of course Father ensured a few competitive games were played. Through my eyes, the family was as happy as it had ever been.

Dad kept himself busy all through his leave period and could put his hand to anything when needed: he upholstered the sofa, made bits of essential furniture, stools in particular.

One day, out came the old iron shoe-last. Dad always repaired shoes when he could get any leather. Imagine our surprise when he took his trusty army knife out, spat on the blade and proceeded to cut a car tyre to pieces. Boots and shoes were quickly repaired, though sometimes with differing depths of tread. This, although embarrassing to us at the time, brought a laugh or two in later life.

Unfortunately nothing lasts forever and Dad had to return to his unit, but not before he'd discovered our debts to the shop and tallyman. He settled these up and Vi promised to be more careful. The last couple of days of my leave saw tears and pleading.

'Can I stay with you, Mum?' I begged, but Dad would not hear of it. He had come to see me back to Waterloo Station.

'You're doing well, son. Keep it up,' said Dad.

'But I don't want to go in the army,' I whined.

'You're too young to know what you want—you'll change your

mind.'

'Don't cry, Bobby,' said Mother, giving me a big hug and with warm tears running down her own face. 'You know I'm always thinking of you.'

With heavy heart and heavy boots, I trudged off after Father, and noticed for the first time the crown above the three stripes on his perfectly pressed uniform.

'Keep up, son, or we'll be late for the train.'

As if I cared.

13

THE TRAIN JOURNEY FROM WATERLOO to Braunton was completed in sombre mood as we realised that our long leave was truly over and school routine was about to begin again. We wondered when we might see our families once more, the optimists plumping for a year's time, the pessimists for after the end of the war, whenever that would be. In the event all were wrong, but we weren't to know that, which was a mixed blessing.

The rain sympathised with our lot in life and poured on us as we disembarked and streamed out of the small station.

'Marlborough over here—get a move on. Roberts, over there—look lively boy.' The rude awakening. I spotted Joe's face as we formed-up in three's but there was no time for talk. We marched off through the rain feeling thoroughly miserable and were soaked to the skin in the first mile. The good news for us all at this point in time was that the hated Pinder had left the school to become a band boy in his father's regiment. No doubt a new bully would emerge but we were in the privileged middle-ground position with nearly three years' service. A new freedom came upon us.

It took some time to settle down to discipline after six weeks at home, but I was pleased to see my pal Alf again.

Poor old Alf the Cockney hadn't been on leave, as he was an orphan with no close relatives. Nevertheless he was a cheerful character, sharp as a button, slim and agile and always ready with a quick reply. Many boys had stayed behind for one reason or another. The school had arranged for them to work on local farms and Alf seemed quite happy as he earned quite a bit of money, and the farmer's wife had mothered him. Both Joe and I were to be grateful to Alf's adopted mother in the months ahead.

Joe, Alf and I—the three musketeers—had moved to different classes, were more worldly-wise and getting tougher and craftier all the time.   Schooling stepped up a pace and, as well as a complete secondary education together with technical and military training, we started gunnery and signalling. The trade of bandsman continued plus all sports. Dear Dusty Miller still tried to breed his champions. Within two weeks things were back to normal.

Sunday Church Parade was compulsory for everybody. There isn't a Dukie alive who could not recite verbatim the school hymn:

> Oh Lord, thy banner floateth o'er us,
> Beneath its folds we stand and sing!
> In majesty go thou before us,
> Our Saviour Christ! Our Captain King!
> Sons of the Brave! Our hearts now hail Thee
> Bravest of all! And cry to Thee:
> Oh Lord, make us Thy faithful soldiers,
> And lead us on—to Victory.

It was a very moving hymn and evoked a response in all of us. The boys may have become tough, hard, many independent and worldly, but firm, strong friendships were made, and there was pride and a great sense of belonging in being a Dukie.

The school song was sung regularly and was very moving. It helped build pride and team spirit. So the months rolled by. Letters from Mum were quite worrying as the Germans were bombing daily and Brentwood was getting a few left-overs. I worried about my family more now. Before going on leave I had no idea of how near they were to London and also I hadn't realised how difficult rationing had made life for Mother.

No-one knew when the war would end, everyone had given up hoping "by Christmas," we couldn't see an end to it, no-one could, so everyone came to accept it and just carry on making the best of things.

Weekends were always the best.   Time off on Saturday afternoon to go nosing around the neighbourhood, or over the hills to Croyde Bay to search, and pinch from, the few wooden chalets on the fringe of the sand dunes. Other times we'd play hide and seek in the fields and hedgerows or go down to Braunton if we had enough cash.

We were roaming on one cool Saturday afternoon in October, just the three of us as always, the inseparable three.

'That's a funny place for a balloon,' said Joe picking it up off

105

the dry stone wall. 'Ugh,' he said, shaking his fingers to get rid of the thing. 'It's all sticky.'

'That ain't a balloon; it's a French letter,' said Alf, laughing. 'Garn!' replied Joe scornfully. 'You can't write on that.'

Alf was in hysterics and I didn't know what to think.

'You don't write on it—you put it on your willie to stop having a baby,' guffawed the worldly Alf.

'You're kidding—men don't have babies,' said Joe.

Alf was now rolling on his back in laughter.

'What a pair of twerps—never seen a French letter.' He then went on to crudely explain the facts of life to the amazed and unbelieving Joe and me.

'Bunk!' said Joe. 'You're making it up; nobody would do things like that.'

As the weeks went by the harvest of balloons increased rapidly on bushes, dry stone walls and cliff tops. The Yanks were leaving their trademark everywhere and it became a game on Saturdays as to who could count the most.

One such Saturday, just next to the hotel, and only thirty yards from the cliff edge, Joe and I were closely studying a new style pink balloon hanging on a protruding stone in a dry stone wall, when I noticed a gap between the stones and a box between two layers of wall. We quickly removed a few loose stones and found a full box of small bars of toilet soap. We couldn't believe our luck. The outside bars were a bit messy but the others were as new. We filled our pockets and secreted the rest back in the wall. Another luxury item was added to the shop that night at twopence a bar. We searched the dry stone walls for the next few Saturdays but no more treasures were found. Those weeks of repetitive routine soon had Christmas upon us, and the school staged its annual show for those few parents who were near enough to attend, together with local dignitaries.

I found myself with the part of Bottom in a shortened version of *A Midsummer Night's Dream*. My acceptance of the part was to placate Beaker Parker in the hope of gaining respite for my ears and backside.

A hole cut in the middle of a sheet and draped over my head was all the costume I got. 'A crack—a crack—I spy a crack,' was the line that sticks in my memory.

The show had a lighter side as well and I was thought to have a good French accent. Against my will, but to save having my ears pulled off, I agreed to recite a poem. *Toute Epine a sa Rose*—every thorn has its rose. It was about flowers, cornfields and eagles. The show was a great success and a few brownie points were chalked up for me with the authorities, but these were soon used up and forgotten as we moved through 1944.

Cockney Alf had taken Joe and me to his friendly farm on a number of occasions and, God bless the farmer's wife, we were always given something to eat. We often did a few small jobs or at least offered to, but the worldly lady knew we were mercenary beggars and had really come for a feed. The farm was quite a way from the school, nearly three miles toward Croyde Bay. We traversed the hill and across the fields to get there—sometimes varying our route for nosy reasons or because fields were full of animals that we didn't fancy getting too close to.

On one such detour on a sunny Saturday afternoon, we topped a knoll and looked down the valley as Alf said,

'Look at that poor bleedin' 'orse,' pointing to a field to the left and below us.

The horse seemed to be stuck to a post. All three of us ran down the hill, through two fields and were now close enough to see what was wrong. A stout pole was fixed in the ground in the centre of the field. The horse had been tethered on a long rope to the pole. The silly animal had gone round in circles, the rope getting shorter all the time, until it ended up where it was now, its head right next to the post and it couldn't move. The animal hadn't the sense to back off or go the opposite way.

'You two stay still,' I said. 'I know all about horses—my Dad's in the cavalry.'

I had seen my father approach horses in a hundred different situations and now did a passable imitation of him. Moving forward slowly and talking softly all the time, I approached the horse. The horse's ears were pricked up and it stood alert as I drew near. I—somewhat nervously—stroked its flank and continued my soft chatter. After a minute or so I gently backed the horse off the post and started to walk him in the opposite direction to untangle the rope. The horse was gentle and put up no resistance.

Joe and Alf joined me and the horse seemed to like the company. It was Alf who noticed; I was too busy whispering to it.

'The poor bugger's blind,' he said.

The shock of the statement brought proceedings to a halt. I moved my hand in front of the horse's eyes, no flinching—the eyes didn't move. We were stunned and very upset.

Sharp old Alf went on to state, 'That's why the poor bugger's on a stake and not running free.'

We left the horse having first named him "Duke" and promised to come back and see him. A plan was devised to visit and feed Duke as often as we could and, if possible during the week—maybe on cross-country runs. The food for Duke was obtained by rifling the swill bins at the back of the kitchens. Little was I to know that caring for Duke set in train the downfall of a Dukie and possibly a notable army career.

Tragedy occurred at the school towards the end of 1944. A boy lost his arm apparently picking up a hand grenade, and within a short space of time another boy lost a hand and an eye whilst playing by the cliffs. This brought home to everyone the dangers now lurking around the dunes and cliffs. Trips to the Yanks were definitely off.

As Christmas approached I was admitted to Exeter hospital to have my tonsils out and remember hiding under the bed-clothes at visiting times. All the other local kids had their parents visiting and my thoughts were with Mum and Dad as I lay in the dark, crying softly. I felt terribly left out. The week on my own seemed to last forever and I was pleased to get out of that lonely place.

14

UNKNOWINGLY, I WAS NOW ENTERING a period of great personal change. The flaws in my character were going to earn me full retribution. Pain would re-enter my life and change its course drastically. Self inflicted wounds are the hardest to bear and tend to influence one's whole outlook. This is how character is formed, by experience, both good and bad. And what lay ahead, all unforeseen, was very bad indeed.

Returning from hospital I soon took up my old pursuits and being one of the older boys, became a little complacent. The three musketeers took it in turns to forage the swill bins for their pet horse Duke.

One Friday night it was my turn again and after lights out, I descended the stairs and made my way round the hotel to the kitchens with two large paper bags—one inside the other—to get Duke's Saturday meal. The bins were in a row outside the rear door of the kitchen. I quietly and quickly filled my bag with bread, cabbage and anything else I could find and was about to leave when I noticed the rear door to the kitchen was open. The dim bulb in the corridor threw just enough light for me to see some cardboard cartons stacked against the wall—obviously delivered too late to be securely locked away in the food store.

Closer examination showed the cartons to contain individually boxed Lyons fruit pies. These square pies were sometimes served as pudding with Sunday lunch, when they were cut into four pieces and each boy got a quarter with watery custard—the treat of the week.

With no thought to the consequences if I got caught, I stuffed six pies, each in its small box, up my tunic and made my way back upstairs.

I was so excitedly anticipating my room mates' reaction to sharing the pies that my normal caution was forgotten. Usually I stopped and listened at the bottom of each flight of stairs, but not this time.

As I hurried up the stairs with Duke's bag of food in one hand and my other arm across my waist holding in the six boxed pies, I could have dropped dead with shock when a loud voice shouted, 'Stand still that boy—stand still I say!'

Looking up the stairwell I saw R.S.M. Bailey glaring down at me.

I stood in the half light trembling with fear, as the R.S.M. descended the stairs—never taking his eyes off me. The school was deathly quiet. Almost midnight, out of bounds, caught red-handed—there was nothing I could do.

'Name and number, boy,' he barked.

'Freeman, M34, sir.'

Stand to attention, boy, when I address you.'

I instinctively brought my hands down to my sides and out of my tunic tumbled four of the six Lyons pies.

Theft was an unforgivable crime in the Dukies and was always punished by a birching in public. The whole school had to parade to watch it. I had witnessed two such birchings in my four years at the school.

Charged before the Commandant with stealing six Lyons pies—Duke's food was forgotten—I couldn't summon a word in my defence. The Commandant was strict as one would expect under a military regime with three hundred and sixty boys to control. I stood to attention in front of his desk, shaking. He peered over his glasses at me.

'I had great hopes for you, son, representing the Dukies at boxing, regularly in the marching band and good educational results'—I had just passed my exam for the Army Military School—Second Class Certificate—'and now you have thrown it all away. I cannot be lenient with you—you know the penalty for stealing. Subject to the medical officer—six strokes—take him away—punishment at two pm today.'

You could get up to twelve strokes if the medical officer thought the prisoner was strong enough so I was lucky, if that's what you call getting six strokes of the birch.

The memory of it will never leave me.

All the boys and military staff were assembled in rows in the main assembly hall, leaving a clear, elongated area in the middle of the room. A solid table took up centre position.

C.S.M. Halyard's grip on my left arm tightened as we entered and the sight of so many faces, all eyes pitying and focusing on me, sapped all the remaining energy from my body. I could barely stand.

'Soon be over, son,' whispered the C.S.M.

We may have stood there a minute or an hour for all I know before the R.S.M. strode in carrying the long birch. My heart was pounding. Panic convulsed me as the Commandant entered behind the R.S.M. The only noise was the wind lashing rain on the windows. Hardly anyone moved.

'School—school, attention,' barked the R.S.M.

The Commandant slowly surveyed the silent audience as I struggled to gain control of my limbs. Then he looked at the R.S.M. and nodded.

'School—school, stand at ease,' barked the R.S.M.

The Commandant again slowly examined the rows of faces before speaking—then he looked at me.

'The honour of our glorious school has been brought into disrepute and blackened.'

Again the long silent pause—the scrutiny of frightened faces.

'The unforgivable crime of theft besmirches this institution's famous name.'

He allowed each sentence to hang in the air. My body was wet with fear as the C.S.M. held on to me.

'No punishment can erase the slur on this school's reputation.' Another pause. 'This wretched boy—M34 Freeman—is a thief.'

The Commandant's eyes burnt into me.

'Theft, the most heinous of crimes, will always be rewarded with maximum punishment. You will witness that punishment, and remember it! Carry on R.S.M.'

I was now totally out of control—sheer panic had gripped me.

'School—school attention! C.S.M. Halyard, prisoner to the table,' barked R.S.M. Bailey

The C.S.M. dragged me towards the table. Bending his head he tried to whisper, 'Be brave, son, soon be over,' but the R.S.M. heard.

'C.S.M.' he clipped.

My tunic was removed and the C.S.M. pulled my khaki shirt and vest well clear of the waistline. When this was done, the R.S.M. snapped 'Senior boys advance.'

Four senior boys marched forward and took up positions at

each corner of the table standing rigidly to attention.

'Take up your positions,' barked the R.S.M.

I was in a tearful daze. Everything seemed to be going in slow motion.

C.S.M. Halyard's quiet voice said, 'Lie across the table, son—courage now.'

'Use commands C.S.M., if you please,' barked the R.S.M.

I was forced across the table, face down. Two senior boys took a leg each and pulled outwards and downwards bending my legs around the table sides. The other two gripped an arm apiece. All four pulled tightly. Suddenly I was blind with tears. The C.S.M. passed round the table and took my head in his hands. He turned my head ninety degrees to the right, holding one hand behind my head and one under the chin.

I stared at the sea of faces, blinking away tears but as my eyes met others they turned away. I saw both Alf and Joe standing together and Joe had tears running down his face.

I was spread-eagled and helpless, I couldn't move. The R.S.M. adjusted one boy's position and grip as I lay there terrified.

'Brace yourselves boys—tighten up.'

The boys pulled harder and at last the R.S.M. was satisfied.

I tried to remember what happened when I'd watched two others get punished—then I heard the *swoosh*. Practice swings—that's what he was doing. He always did three or four. Was it for effect—to frighten the audience who were now fidgeting uncomfortably? The second swoosh through the huge arc of the swing produced a high pitched screaming noise. Two more faster and louder as I lie pinned—past panic, past terror—petrified.

Then the tap on the bum. I knew what he was doing—I remembered now. He was measuring the long, split ended birch from its tip on my backside to his standing position. Next he would retreat three long paces—then come forward quickly—the swoosh would go to scream—and that would be the first blow.

Suddenly there was a thump and whispering broke out. I blinked my eyes rapidly to be able to see what was happening. I was so tensed-up—waiting for the first stroke. A boy had fainted.

'Remove that boy,' commanded the R.S.M. irritably.

The boy was removed by the staff and my nightmare continued as the R.S.M. made another practice swing before once more starting to measure his distance.

After he tapped my backside again only the lashing rain could

112

be heard as I waited in dread. At last I heard his foot movement—the high pitched scream of the birch—and then it happened. CRACK. The most excruciating pain blazed deep into my buttocks, throbbing pain—like frozen hands plunged into hot water—thumped down my legs and up the centre of my back.

My head nearly exploded; my legs seemed to drop off; the table jumped forward a foot as my body convulsed under the first blow.

'Hold tight boys, hold tight,' growled the R.S.M.

I couldn't remember whether I screamed; I only remembered the second stroke and thought my whole body was breaking in pieces. I must have passed out after that. Never was I to experience such pain ever again in my life. After all such birchings the prisoner was carried to the sickbay, and that's where I came to.

It was five days before I could walk and then not too steadily. Three days were spent lying on my stomach having my bleeding backside treated. The weals across my buttocks could be seen quite distinctly nine months later.

C.S.M. Halyard visited me every day in the sickbay and was a very kind, sympathetic man: coming to the end of his long army career and carrying out orders that he hadn't really got the heart for.

My predecessors had to suffer further indignity as the history books show. A boy could have a log chained to his ankle for two days or more. He had to drag this with him throughout the school. This punishment was supposed to deter boys from being caught out-of-bounds. At least I missed that one.

The practice of birching was banned from all schools by law in 1948.

My return to my friends in the April of 1945 found both sympathy and respect, but the experience had changed my life. Poor Duke, the blind horse, was never seen again. I'd had plenty of time to think, lying in the sickbay for days in great pain. Life up to then had been something of a game. I was the first to recognise that I had got away with murder over the years and that finally it had caught up with me. No way was I going to go into the Army after this. I was going to get out of the Dukies, come hell or high water.

C.S.M. Halyard had encouraged me to attend Bible lessons at his bungalow so that I could be confirmed. I had started these lessons in the January of 1945 and in April the brutal birching had taken place. It took some persuasion by the C.S.M. to get me to see the lessons through, but I did that out of respect for him and his caring wife.

I was confirmed by the Lord Bishop of Exeter on the 13th June 1945 and in the prayer book given to me, the Bishop wrote my personal prayer: 'Use me, O Lord, and make me fit to be used.'

God would have a hard time doing that, I thought.

I wrote home and told Father I wanted out. Dad replied (he didn't know about the birching and I hadn't mentioned it): 'We all go through bad patches in life, son—stick it out a bit longer and see how you get on.' Mother had given birth to baby Roger—the eighth Freeman—in April and the new baby was the main topic in Dad's letter.

And so it was that I was left to soldier on. Father could have got me out of the Dukies if he had wanted to, but it seemed there was no desire on his part to bring me back into the family fold.

I was feeling bitter again, and that didn't bode well for the school or for me.

15

THE WAR IN EUROPE ENDED with Germany's unconditional surrender in May 1945 and Japan followed suit in August. The Dukies were to vacate the hotel at Saunton Sands and return to their permanent school at Dover by the end of the year. We were sent home on leave and told to report to the school's pre-war home at Lone Tree Hill, Dover, on our return.

I arrived home to much rejoicing and saw my new baby brother for the first time. Rationing was still as severe as ever and Mother looked poorly. The family was still living in Britannia Road, Warley and Father hadn't been transferred any nearer home and was still stationed in Surrey.

I had two things in mind: one, to persuade Father to get me released from the Dukies and two, to ensure neither Mother or family ever saw my backside which was now covered in dark brown lines slightly indented into grooves.

The whole country was seething with happiness. The war's end had seen many families re-united for the first time in many years. Life was on a high for most people. No more doodle-bugs, no more air-raid sirens. No longer was it necessary to carry the cardboard boxes with the ill-fitting gas masks inside. There was even talk of rationing ending soon. In fact rationing continued right through to 1950, with a few items still rationed in 1953. Even bread was rationed, for the first time, *after* the war. We had defeated our enemies, now we had to pay for the victory.

Number Four, Britannia Road, was all dressed up for the festive season. It wasn't Christmas in our house unless the front room—or the living room—ceilings simply couldn't be seen. Mother pinned criss-cross decorations across every conceivable space and draped more colourful paper chains round mirrors and pictures. There was always a bright garland over the mantelpiece. An explosion of colour greeted the many neighbours who popped in for a quick one over the Christmas period.

Many of the decorations were made by the family sitting round the fire of an evening, prior to Christmas. Paper chains were the most common and easy to make. We had fun slopping the flour and water paste over everything, including ourselves; Mother tried to scold us, but laughed at the same time. Those were happy times indeed, for Father was also home.

The major presents for the boys would be made by Father at his carpentry lessons in Surrey. Mother would have knitted jumpers and socks often unpicking old woollies to re-use the wool. She was an excellent and very fast knitter and produced most if not all the woollies for the family. At one time Mother knitted three identical cable-stitch pullovers for Father, Vic and me and they were all works of art.

Father was a good cook and always helped to prepare Christmas lunch. He was also a good organiser and the boys were given bowls of vegetables to peel and clean. Christmas was a family affair and we all joined in as the radio blared seasonal music incessantly.

Father made the stuffing for the bird, Vic got a friendly clip for pinching a mince pie—intended for tea-time—and shoving the whole pie in his mouth at one go, and grinning at Mum as his cheeks stuck out like an orang-utan's. We stuffed ourselves with anything going, with no thought for the morrow—which maybe wasn't a bad thing in the circumstances.

Vic often asked, 'What's for tea, Mum?'

'Ifits,' she always replied.

'What's that, Mum?'

'If it's bread and jam, its bread and jam. If it's Spam, it's Spam.' And she would always laugh and we were none the wiser.

Father always slept off his dinner on Christmas Day, so the front room was out of bounds. After tea he would arrange games for the whole family. "Pinning the tail on the donkey" was the favourite. He would draw a donkey on a blackboard and make a cardboard tail. One at a time and blindfolded, we had to walk the length of the front room—all the furniture had been moved back—and pin the cardboard tail on the donkey on the blackboard. We all laughed so much and it was great fun.

To really enjoy Christmas one needs a big family around and things are never quite the same from generation to generation. My childhood memories of Christmas are memories of really happy times.

Christmas was soon over and my leave was only for two weeks. Everything has to end sometime and I was due to return to the Dukies in January 1946. My pleading to Father had fallen on deaf ears, and although I had heard Mother plead my case, Dad would have none of it. It was back to Military School for me and no more arguments.

I had been too frightened of Dad's reaction to tell him or Mother of my flogging. Dad wouldn't take kindly to knowing that I was a thief. The fact that I had stolen food to share with mates who were always as hungry as I was would have been hard for either Mum or Dad to believe. The Army looked after its own. As for the strict regime, well, discipline never hurt anyone, and bullying just couldn't happen in a disciplined environment. I knew all of Father's answers. Tears were of no avail as he took me to the railway station.

'He will be home more often now,' said Fred to Vi, 'and I will call in to see him now and again, now that he's going to be at Dover.'

So I went back to the Dukies at their peacetime home.

The school was built high on the white cliffs, four hundred feet above sea level and within sight of Dover Castle. There were two entrances to the school on the main road with a keeper's cottage at each one. A wall skirted the boundary.

The focal point of the school was the large dining hall with its dominating clock-tower. Eight H shaped single-storey buildings, four each side, led off from the dining hall and these were the eight Houses—previously Companies—of the school.

Three legs of each H building housed the boys in long dormitories of twenty-four iron beds—each with a wooden trunk at the foot. The fourth leg of the H was the C.S.M.'s quarters and the centre of the H was the dayroom.

The school had its own church, library, schoolrooms and vast playing fields. What I found on arrival could not have been more disappointing. Cockney Alf had left, withdrawn by his guardians. Little was I to know, until years later, that Alf had been adopted by the friendly farmer and his wife, and that we were to meet up again in happier circumstances. My best friend Joe had been transferred to another House.

Both my friends were gone and there were many new faces all round as numbers had swelled to over five hundred boys now that those who had been evacuated to Dumblane School in Scotland had returned to Dover. The worst news of all was that C.S.M. Halyard had retired. A new and younger C.S.M. was now in charge of my House and without doubt he had it in for me.

It must be surmised that the new C.S.M. had read his brief and done his homework. He must have been aware—or so I reasoned—that M34 Freeman was the only boy in his House to have been birched. From day one I could do nothing right. Everything had to be done two or three times; it didn't matter how well I cleaned the toilets and showers, or how neatly I folded my bedding or greatcoat, it was, in the eyes of the C.S.M., 'Not good enough. Do it again, boy.'

I was convinced the C.S.M. was out to break me. Fatigues and extra duties became a way of life and I had to take all the C.S.M. could throw at me.

Each year the school had a "Grand Day"—trooping the colour, and prize-giving. That year, 1946, it was to be extra special as Field Marshal Viscount Montgomery of Alamein was to take the salute and be the guest of honour. Grand Day was to take place in June, rehearsals and band practices were stepped up and the whole school's attention was focused forward.

I was performing, day to day, like a robot, miserable without my friends, extra duties all the time, and still set on leaving the Dukies and returning to my family.

Mother was writing regularly and out of the blue she sent me a parcel, the first and only time she ever did. I was delighted. The new C.S.M. made me open it in front of the other boys and saw me take out of the cardboard box a feather pillow in grey and black striped material. The pillow had been doubled over to protect a home-made fruit cake and I was, of course, over the moon with the surprise. Just what I needed to buck me up a bit.

I was totally unprepared for what happened next.

The C.S.M. decreed the cake would be shared between all the boys present and sent for a knife. The cake was soon devoured. He then confiscated the feather pillow and it was never seen again.

'Against regulations, Freeman. A bolster is what you've got.'

I had reached the bottom of my unhappy existence and could take no more. In desperation I decided that night to run away. Where, I didn't know. Plans—I had none.

After lights out and when everyone was asleep, I dressed quietly, my heart pounding, picked up my boots and greatcoat and tiptoed out of the dormitory and made off.

It was a dark and cold night as I climbed the school wall, dropped to the grass below and started to jog towards St. Margaret's Bay. I knew they would look for me in Dover so I went in the opposite direction.

I walked and jogged all through the night, leaving the main road and taking off across the fields. I had no idea where I was going.

Passing through a small village as dawn was breaking, I pinched a cardboard-topped pint of milk from a doorstep and put it in my greatcoat pocket. Leaving the village behind, as daylight started to creep across the landscape, I made for a haystack in the corner of a field. I soon made a big hole at the bottom and crept in, drank my milk and fell off to sleep, thoroughly exhausted.

When I woke up, I was frightened and only then did it dawn on me what I had done. I had no idea where I was and no watch to tell the time of day. I sat huddled up wondering what would become of me and had a good cry. I learnt later that Father and the local police had been informed; he went to the school to await news.

I had no idea how long I sat in the haystack, but eventually I ventured out and continued skirting the fields, always keeping to the hedgerows and cutting through copses. I was starving but could find nothing to eat. Darkness fell.

I hadn't seen a single human being all day, just a car passing along a lane in the distance. Cold, tired and hungry I was past caring about anything as I crossed a muddy farmyard and knocked on a kitchen door.

A dog started to bark and I stood there cold and scared. The door opened, splaying a beam of light over my bedraggled form. I was half-blinded by the light from within. A ruddy-faced man looked down at the soldier boy.

'What have we here? Martha, come and look. Where have you come from, son, at this time of night?'

I had difficulty in finding my voice and before I could reply the farmer's wife appeared. 'Don't keep him there, Jeff. Come in, son, you look frozen to death.'

The farmer's wife soon had me sitting by a roaring fire and quickly made a bowl of soup.

'Don't question the boy, Jeff. Time enough for that later. He looks frightened out of his life, poor little thing.'

Fed and warmed through, the story was soon told. The farmer

rang the local police and, at his wife's suggestion, got them to agree to leave me where I was until morning as it was then ten-thirty at night. I was put to bed and had no trouble falling asleep as I was totally drained of energy.

The police took me back to school next morning and to my surprise Father—who had stayed overnight—wasn't angry.

'I'll get you released, son; I've talked to the C.O. and your C.S.M. but it may take two or three weeks.'

I suppose they had told Dad about the birching and that was the reason for his softer attitude towards me. But I am sure my Mother was never told for she would never have been able to hide it from me. My brothers and sister certainly never knew.

There was to be no punishment; I was lectured by the C.O. and if I stayed on my best behaviour, I would be home with my family within a month. It was now the beginning of June 1946.

My last parade was Grand Day! I played in the band for trooping the colour and marched past the famous General. Life has a funny way of turning a complete circle and, stranger than fiction, I was to end up a few years later looking after Monty's personal DC Dakota.

One week to the day after trooping the colour, Father collected me from the Dukies and re-united me with my family. A stranger, a misfit—what would the future hold for me in Civvy Street? Only time would tell.

16

BY JULY 1946, THE SECOND WORLD WAR had been over for almost a year and that great end-of-war euphoria was long gone. The overall quality of life was not good. About half of the men in the Forces had returned to civvy street but not to a land flowing in milk and honey. Because of bomb damage, there was a severe housing shortage, just at a time when thousands of demobbed men were wanting to marry. At the same time rationing was still in force, not only of food, but also of clothing. Almost everything was in short supply, even cigarettes, and male unemployment was rising. Many factories geared to the war effort had closed down and women who were now used to doing men's jobs wouldn't give up their income. This was the grumbling and grousing era. Everyone expected a return to pre-war normality long before twelve months had elapsed after the end of hostilities, with food and jobs in abundance; they got neither.

It was decided I was too old—fourteen years seven months—to start schooling again, so I reported to the Labour Exchange at the bottom of Brentwood High Street.

The High Street stretched for a mile, with rows of shops on both sides. There were two picture houses in the centre, almost opposite one another, the Odeon and the Plaza. Burtons the Tailors was next to the Odeon with a snooker hall above it. Vic and I spent many hours in the next twelve months on one of the sixteen tables learning the game and becoming skilled at it.

Mother was still working part-time at her war-time job in the local British Restaurant situated in a side road by Brentwood and Warley railway station. British Restaurants, a pretentious name for a nationwide chain of state-controlled cheap canteens, served subsidised standard lunches at tenpence for two courses. Mum worked in the kitchens and one of the perks of the job was that she could take her youngest children with her. Also, from time to time, a few bits and pieces of foodstuffs came home to supplement the rations.

Vic was now sixteen and had grown into a broad-shouldered, muscular young man. He worked on building sites, one of the main opportunities for employment immediately after the war. He had an enormous appetite and Mother would use nearly a whole loaf of bread making his lunchtime sandwiches. He had also joined a local band and played drums. Vic was physically different from me. Whereas I had shot up to five feet five inches and was as skinny as a rake, Vic was slightly shorter, had broad shoulders and was two stones heavier.

Ernie was now ten years old and attending the local primary school at Warley. He was to turn out to be the brainy one of the family and went on to attend Romford Technical College and eventually became qualified as a chartered structural engineer.

Pauline was eight years old and accompanied Ernie to the local primary school. She was the apple of our eye and woe betide anyone who did her wrong.

Baby Roger—just a year old—never left Mother's sight.

I soon settled into the family routine and found time on my hands in the first few weeks, as everyone disappeared each morning to their various pursuits.

While I was waiting for the Labour Exchange to find me a job, I would wander down to Mum's restaurant for my free lunch. Passing by the railway station one Tuesday morning I saw a notice 'AUCTION THIS WAY.' Following the signs I came upon an old railway building and crowds of people. Outside the building were job lots that were in the sale. Old wardrobes jostled tables, tatty sofas, bicycles, various cardboard boxes full of crockery and ornaments, even kitchen sinks. It seemed anything that would fetch a shilling was put in the sale, each with a numbered label.

There were crowds of people milling around, poking at furniture and trying the bikes. I was fascinated and wandered inside the shed. My eyes opened wide as I saw rows of hutches with rabbits for sale, canaries in cages, chickens in pens.

'Sale about to start,' shouted a cloth-capped, brown-coated man. 'Outside everybody,' and I was ushered out into the open with the crowd.

Well above the throng, on a table, stood the auctioneer, a man of cheerful appearance also wearing a cloth cap and brown overall. He held a clip of papers on a board in his left hand and a pen in his right as he called for order.

'Lot one,' he shouted, 'a fine oak sideboard. Who'll start at two pounds?' Complete silence—'Thirty bob then.' A squeaky voice from the left said, 'Twenty-two and sixpence.'

'Somebody thinks it's his birthday,' said the jovial auctioneer and the crowd laughed. 'I have twenty-two and six—do I hear more?' So I experienced my first of many auctions.

During the war years only Government sponsored utility furniture was manufactured, designed with simple lines to make the most of scarce raw materials. It was well-made but unpopular, lacking the opulent highly polished appearance of cheap, pre-war mass-production. In any case, it wasn't readily available. One had to be bombed out to obtain it. Any furniture at all sold readily in the early years after the war.

The following Tuesday I arrived at the auction early and had a good look round. I was earning seven shillings and sixpence a week from my morning paper round and, after giving Mum half a crown, I had five shillings left for my own use. There were lots of cardboard boxes containing bric-a-brac and I saw a butter dish I was sure Mum would like—not that we ever had butter—but it would do for Sunday tea, I thought, to put the margarine in. I waited patiently until Lot 69 came up. No bidders at first, so I held back.

My heart was thumping for some reason as I said, 'Sixpence,' and put my hand up. The auctioneer had to look to find where the voice had come from.

'Sixpence I have from the bright-eyed youngster—do I hear more?'

Usually others are waiting for someone to start before they join in, but there wasn't a great enthusiasm for Lot 69. It crept up a penny a time and I obtained my box for one and tuppence.

The box was carried home up Warley Hill with some excitement. The butter dish was washed and looked lovely. It was a china dish with a maroon and brown willow pattern. Mum was delighted with her present and this made me very happy. The rest of the bric-a-brac was washed, placed back in the box on clean newspapers and re-entered in the following Tuesday's auction—it fetched two shillings. I had found another sideline but unfortunately it didn't always make a profit.

The first few weeks of civvy street, back in the family bosom, were nice but strange. I found it difficult to settle. For one thing I

123

was suffering from nightmares. The same dream kept recurring—I was back in the Dukies, standing in the main assembly hall surrounded by a sea of faces and with hundreds of eyes boring into me.

In my dream, the birch was twice as large and the R.S.M. was much bigger and had a grotesque face. The dream continued to the first blow when I would wake up in various positions, covered in sweat.

Paradoxically, there were periods during the day I thought of Joe and Alf and wished we were together.

When you look back, you always remember the good times but also miss the deep friendships forged from shared hardships. For me, the camaraderie and the sense of belonging had gone. I was finding it difficult at times to adjust to civilian life after five long years of regimented existence.

One morning, whilst delivering papers up Woodman Road, I noticed a card in a window of the last house next to Selo's factory. Selo's was the nickname given by the locals to the Ilford Film Company which produced rollfilm with the Selochrome trade-name for all types of cameras. The notice said, 'BOY WANTED—APPLY WITHIN.' I couldn't finish my paper-round quick enough and was soon back knocking on the front door.

'Go round the back,' said a miserable-looking woman.

I couldn't see a back door, only two eight foot high boarded gates that had, many years before, been painted green. They were now in a decaying state, peeling or with no paint at all, the lower part of them rotted away. The gates were shut, so I knocked. There was no reply to the feeble noise I made. I picked a stone up from the gutter and banged on the gates.

'I'm coming!' a mournful voice complained and a chain rattled.

The gate drew back and a man stood there looking down at me. Mr Mellows was fiftyish, scruffy as a tramp, big and heavy-looking with a fat face that hadn't seen a razor for at least two days. His dirty and torn baggy trousers were tucked into cut-down gum boots. A hacking jacket that had seen better days was tied around his waist with string. He had nothing on his balding head. I was immediately frightened of him.

'Come for the job, have you, son?' he said. 'Look a bit puny to me for this job.'

'Oh no, sir, I'm strong,' I said, more scared now of not getting the job than of the man.

'Well—we'll see. I'll give you a day or two and see what you're like—come with me.'

As we walked across the cobbled yard I had time to look around. A dirty old fifteen hundredweight van painted green was parked between piles of secondhand timber. A storage tank stood on a framework of four foot high angle iron. Five-gallon drums seemed to be everywhere. A wooden mangle propped up two rusty bikes. We soon entered a ramshackle shed and I saw my first bundles of firewood neatly stacked to one side. Mr Mellows flopped his huge body into a sawdust-covered old armchair and, for the first time, smiled at me.

'Right, lad,' he started. 'We go out with the van on Thursday, Friday and Saturday and sell our wares—soap, soap powders and flakes, firewood and paraffin. I've got a good round—you'll soon pick it up. Monday and Tuesday we chop wood and make nice bundles—all the same,' he pointed to those stacked nearby. 'Soap's on coupons and don't you forget it—all right?' So I started my first job.

That night Mum had her first session of picking the wood splinters out of my hands and knitted me some thick mittens for protection within a week.

Defying his appearance, Mr Mellows turned out to be quite a friendly chap although his wife was a frosty old woman. The first couple of days on the road were enjoyable, knocking on doors. 'Want any paraffin or wood, missus?' Lots of women gave me a cake or some titbit and it was a healthy and interesting life.

As the van toured the streets, I had to sit amongst the goods, legs dangling over the back of the van, van doors wide open. On one side was a large container of paraffin with the brass tap protruding out over the road so one could fill the cans. On the other side were shelves with Rinso and Persil in packets. To the rear was a sack of Lux flakes, sold by the pound. The back of the van was stacked with firewood, Lifebuoy soap and carbolic.

I soon got used to the smell and the daily routine. On return to base it was my job to stock up for the next day and count and record the soap coupons.

On the first Saturday of my new job I was surprised to see my boss had shaved; he looked a new man.

'Finish early today, Bob,' he smiled.

Good, I thought, I'm going to the pictures tonight to see *The Jolson Story* again. I'd seen it seven times altogether and got upset every time he sang *Sonny Boy.*

Saturday's round was down Orchard Park. I knew the Warley district and all the roads around Selo's very well from my paper rounds, but this was new.

About eleven o'clock the van turned into another side road and Mr Mellows got out of the cab and came to the back.

'Give me six bundles of wood, Bob,' he said, as he took a large packet of Persil and a large Rinso from the shelves, plus a Reckitt's blue bag. 'I'm going to number fourteen; you go up and down the street to the others—and then wait for me—I'm going to have a cup of tea,' and off he went.

It took me a full half hour to do the rest of the street but my boss still wasn't back. I supposed he was having a second cup.

Ten minutes later he returned—all smiles.

'OK, Bob, one more street and then home.'

As it was Saturday, and there was no round until Thursday, it wasn't necessary to restock the van. All I had to do was count the soap coupons; then I could be off.

'Have you got the coupons for the large Persil and Rinso from number fourteen, Mr Mellows?' I asked innocently.

'Um—no, lad—forget 'em—get 'em next week, OK?'

Next week came—Saturday, shaving day. Same routine but this time Mr Mellows was nearly an hour at the house in the side road. As I counted the soap coupons that Saturday afternoon Mr Mellows beat me to the question.

'Before you ask about coupons from number fourteen I don't take 'em off 'er—she's a poor widow woman and it wouldn't be right to ask her—especially as she gives me tea and home-made cakes.' I never gave it another thought.

Just three weeks with Mr Mellows elapsed before a note arrived from the Labour Exchange. 'Report to Achille Sere for interview,' it said. I was in two minds but Mum said I had to go because it was official.

Achille Sere was a dyer's and cleaner's shop right at the top of Brentwood High Street, on the corner by the traffic lights.

'You look a smart lad, son—can you ride a bike?' said the bespectacled manager.

'Yes, sir.'

It was a pound a week more than Mr Mellows was paying and no chopping firewood or smelling of paraffin and soap all the time, so I accepted the job as delivery boy.

The bicycle was a big, heavy steel affair with a square tubular frame at the front which held a large wicker basket. There was an advertising plate fitted across the frame with the shop's name on it. I could hardly reach the pedals and the seat had to be lowered.

'Start on Monday then, son, and don't be late—eight-thirty sharp.' So off I went, full of excitement to tell Mother.

Britannia Road, Warley, was a very long road that was dissected halfway up by a smaller road. At this cross-road, on one corner, was Miss Outrem's general store and next to the store was a small estate of prefabs, factory-built, quickly erected homes provided by the Government to ease the housing shortage after the war. They were given a ten-year life but many were still occupied twenty-five years later.

On the opposite corner to the store was a large, detached house where the Bradleys lived in poverty, all ten children with their parents. The Cherry Tree Pub was next to the Bradleys' house.

Our house was one of twenty Victorian terrace houses further along, at the very top of the street. They had been taken over for military families because of their close proximity to Warley Army Barracks and were right on the curtilage of the camp. All the other houses in Britannia Road were occupied by civilians.

The local kids used the cross-road corner or the pub yard as their nightly meeting point and I soon got to know local ruffians.

My first friends after leaving the Dukies were the Bradley twins, George and Alan. The twins were still at school although they were a month older than me, and after work and at weekends we would meet up at the cross-roads with the other kids. The Murphy girls lived in the prefabs and they were part of the street corner gang. June was twelve years old and her sister Jill was fourteen.

I had never been in close proximity of girls except for baby Pauline and had never played with them in my whole life. I had never considered girls as playmates and found it strange having them chipping in on conversations and even wanting to join in our games.

George and Alan were amused with my rejection of females; they were rough and ready boisterous lads who, having five sisters, had seen it all and accepted females readily. As the days passed I slowly came to accept that girls, even these hardened tomboys could be good fun to play with.

George and Alan had paper-rounds and Saturday morning jobs,

which ensured they had a small income each. They loved gambling and quickly introduced me to pontoon. We would use the air-raid shelter in their back garden. Two stubs of candle would throw their rings of light on the damp piece of plywood used as a table. We tossed for banker and played for a penny a game. I was soon hooked and found I was a lucky gambler, much to the disappointment of my pals, whose enthusiasm started to wane after a few weeks of regularly losing their money to me.

'Let's go up the barracks and show Bob our secret den,' said George one Saturday afternoon.

'Yeah—let's,' agreed Alan.

A row then ensued with some of the other kids who wanted to come. George would have none of it.

'Bugger off all of you,' said George.

Alan wanted Jill to come but not June—'Because she's only twelve years old and she would tell the secret.'

'No,' said George, 'just us three and don't try and follow, else I'll belt ya.' George being the eldest and the biggest was considered the gang leader and nobody argued.

It was a warm August Saturday afternoon as we rambled through the camp and past the parade ground.

One side of Warley barracks was bordered by a large wood that stretched back for some miles. Cut into the wood from the camp was a commando assault course. Next to this was an open air swimming pool at ground level, and this was the area the three of us made for. Some twenty yards into the wood from the swimming pool George and Alan had constructed their secret den in the centre of a massive clump of rhododendrons. With the help of some packing cases, coconut matting, wire mesh and branches they had created a hide with a concealed entrance. Inside we had wooden planks on the floor, old boxes to sit on and candles to see by. It was quite a place and I instantly recognised that it was a sign of their trust that they had taken me there. I had been accepted as one of them.

We had been sitting in the candlelight, talking quietly when George said, 'Shush,' and put his finger to his lips.

'Not much further, come on,' said a voice.

George kept his finger to his lips and we waited. Twigs snapped; leaves rustled. Someone went past the den: one person . . two . .

The noise receded as George whispered, 'Follow me, but don't

128

make a sound.'

Once out in the fresh air George seemed to be taking his bearings, looking left and right, peering this way and that. We waited. Eventually, he made up his mind and struck off stealthily through the trees and, like apprentice Red Indians, we tiptoed behind him.

After a few minutes of this totally mysterious game George looked back and said, 'Sod it, we've lost them; let's go 'ome.'

Not wanting to show my ignorance I held my question as we back-tracked in the direction of home. We'd been walking in silence when George suddenly stopped dead in his tracks.

'Shush,' he whispered.

I heard a pig grunt and grunt again, interspersed with "Ahs," George was grinning.

What the hell is a pig doing in the woods? I thought as we stood there holding our breath. Grinning George, with finger to lips, waved us forward.

We tiptoed through some trees and peered round a bush at the pig some ten feet away in a hollow.

My eyes and mouth competed to see which could open the widest and at first I couldn't make head nor tail of it.

There she lay, legs wide apart and the soles of her bare feet were beating time at the blue sky above. Her dress was rucked up around her waist. Two snow-white breasts, with pointed, brown buttons in the centre, were glistening in the sunlight. Her eyes were closed and strands of red hair were caught in the sweat of her forehead and stuck to her eyes. She was forcing her head back and mouth wide open as she made rhythmic "ahs" with the grunts of the pig.

The pig was a soldier with a large spotty back and biggest white bum I'd ever seen. His shirt was off and his trousers were round his ankles. He lay between the two white, airborne legs and was pumping away with a vicious stroke. What the hell they were up to I had no idea. At each push toward the ground he grunted. I was baffled but also embarrassed.

I took in the spectacle and was trying to work it out when Alan giggled.

The pig was on his feet in an instant and the woman snapped her legs together like a metal trap and screamed. I stared in amazement and fright at the sheer size of the soldier's tool. It must have been two inches wide, and swayed stiffly like a hypnotised

129

cobra in a snake-charmer's basket. I didn't know whether to laugh or cry.

'You little bastards!' he bellowed, and attempted to run at us. He fell flat on his face as the trousers around his ankles tripped him.

I took off in flight, only to find George way ahead of me and Alan not even in sight. We ran like hares and didn't stop until we were in Britannia Road.

Not wanting to show my ignorance, but, full of curiosity, I asked George if he'd seen them before.

'Lots of 'em,' said George. 'They're always at it, them soldiers.'

'At what?' I said before I could stop myself.

'Shagging,' said George. 'You know, making babies. You don't know nuffin', do ya?' said George.

'I do so,' I said. 'My friend Alf told me about that years ago, and French letters.'

'Don't believe ya,' said George. 'I've seen 'um hundreds of times.'

From that day on, whenever I saw a woman with a big belly or a pram, my first thoughts used to make me blush scarlet if they came near me. I know where you've been, I used to think. Up in those woods with the soldiers!

17

I'D BEEN WORKING AT ACHILLE-SERE, the dyers and cleaners, for two weeks. My legs had recovered from the initial stiffness brought on by continually pedalling for a living and I was used to manoeuvring the front-heavy bicycle through traffic and up narrow alleyways. Deliveries went far afield and I found myself pedalling up and down hills in Great Warley and, in the opposite direction, right out to Hutton. Round trips sometimes covered ten miles or more in all sorts of weather. The manager used to time me and if I wasn't quick enough he would threaten to dock my pay. I was growing tired of him.

One day I leant my bike against a wall. It didn't have a stand attachment so, if there was a pavement, I propped it up on a pedal, otherwise I had to lean it against a wall, as on this occasion. The front wicker basket was difficult to open if the bike was against a wall and, with an armful of blankets or coats, it was sometimes impossible to stop the bike falling over and spilling cleaned clothes all over the pavement. Three such mishaps had already occurred and I'd had to take clothes back to the shop to be cleaned again.

'I'm going to take the cost of this re-cleaning out of your wages on Friday. You're just bloody careless!' said the manager.

'But couldn't I have a bike-stand fitted? They're only just over a pound,' I said for the umpteenth time.

'No, you can't. Other boys manage without them. So can you.'

On Friday afternoon the manager gave me my third week's pay-packet. I opened it once I'd reached Harry's café at the bottom of the High Street, and found I was three shillings short. I went back to the shop.

'Sir, you've made a mistake.'

'That's no mistake,' he said. 'That's for the cost of re-cleaning clothes that you dropped this week. You shouldn't be so bloody careless.'

131

I was fuming; I'd pedalled for miles. Often he sent me out on a hour's run just before I should finish for the day, yet he never offered me extra pay for that.

'You can take your bike home when you're finished,' was all he said; some help that was.

'But that's not fair,' I said. 'If I had a stand the bike wouldn't fall over.'

'You're not getting a stand and that's that—off you go,' he said.

'You can stick your job up your arse then,' I said, as I went out slamming the door.

It gave me great pleasure to look back and see his expression. I felt good and was glad to be rid of the job. But as I got off the 339 bus and walked up Britannia Road in the pouring rain I came down to earth. Now I'd got to tell Mum that I hadn't a job.

It was a cold wet September evening as I walked into the house and met a sight I loved to see.

'Hello, Bobby, how are you, darling?' said Mum, spitting on a flat iron to see if it was hot enough.

The spit sizzled, smoked and jumped clean off the shiny surface, and hid in the cloth peg rug fronting the fireguard. The living room smelt damp in spite of the roaring fire. Mum had two flat irons on the go, one clipped on to the front of the grate getting hot while she used the other one. The three foot high, black mesh, brass-topped fire-guard was covered with underwear and towels that had been ironed, but they were still emitting hazy vapour. The line Mum had strung under the mantelpiece was laden down with more clothes drying off completely after ironing and still Mum had piles on the table in front of her.

Pauline, now eight years old, was sprinkling spots of water on garments that were too dry to iron and rolling them up ready for Mum to deal with when she considered them suitably dampened. Ernie, the brains of the family, was attempting to do his homework on the small wicker table by the window. He always seemed to have a lot of homework. Vic hadn't arrived home from work and he would only stop in the house long enough to eat before he was off out again. Baby Roger was crawling under the table, chasing the red London bus Dad had made him. His mouth was gummed up with the Ministry of Food orange concentrate that Mum still put in his bottle even at one year old. This was the comforting sight of home and family that I valued and appreciated more than any of my brothers.

'I've left me job, Mum,' I said, waiting for her reaction. The ironing continued, up and down, without interruption.

'Never mind, love, I didn't like you out in all weathers, pedalling that big bike,' she said without looking up. 'We'll find you a nice indoor job next week, you wait and see.' Dear old Mum.

On Monday, she came with me to the Labour Exchange. The frosty old clerk looked over his metal framed spectacles and fixed me with his frightening stare. 'Three weeks isn't long to stop in a job, son. Jobs are hard to come by; why did you leave?'

Like a shot Mum was in.

'He couldn't manage that big heavy bike; he's not very strong,' she pleaded.

'Took him long enough to find out,' said misery guts, picking out a postcard from his shoebox file. 'This might suit him,' he said. 'Cake shop, middle of the High Street, need a boy for general duties; take this along with you.' He handed Mum a slip of paper.

The money was a bit less than I'd been getting, but it was a lovely warm shop and smelt terrific. I started on the Wednesday. Filling the shelves with fresh bread and cakes was a lovely job. Sweeping up and cleaning, tidying the yard and loading delivery vans suited me fine.

The serving ladies made a fuss of me and we all got free cakes to eat with our tea breaks and shared what was unsold each evening. I loved taking a box of cakes home to Mum.

As the days slipped by and I talked to the others, the owner came up to me. 'So you grew up surrounded by horses, Robert?'

'Yes, sir, my Dad's in the cavalry,' I said with pride, not knowing what I was letting myself in for.

'Good lad,' he said. 'You like horses then?'

'Oh yes, sir.'

'Well, from Monday I want you to report to my house at Mountnessing. I'll give you the address. You can be my assistant pony groom. Same pay, all right?'

'Yes, sir.'

Bloody hell, I thought, I don't want to be a pony groom, whatever that is, I like the cake shop.

On Monday I took the bus to Brentwood and changed buses for Mountnessing. I was nearly an hour late and ninepence ha'penny the worse off. 'Not a very good start,' said Albert, the head groom and gardener. 'You'll have to do better tomorrow if you want to keep your job.'

'But it costs me sixpence ha'penny more to get here than the shop, and I have to leave home earlier.'

'You accepted the job, son but I'll speak to the guv'nor about your bus fare. Come on, I'll show you the horses.'

The big house had extensive gardens and out-buildings. At the very bottom of the garden was a three stall brick stable. Two horses' heads and a pony's head greeted me as we rounded the corner.

'Right, son, we have to brush and comb the horses every day. Two feed times a day, and mucking out and straw-changing twice a week. You'll soon get used to it. Then there's the bridles and tack. I'll soon show you the ropes,' he said.

Albert was obviously very pleased to see me. Life, he thought, was going to be so much easier.

'I left the mucking-out till you came, so let's get started.'

In gumboots three sizes too big for me and wearing a dirty, brown coat with only one button to hold it together, I joined him in shovelling horse-shit and straw into a wooden wheelbarrow. The barrow's wooden sides had been extended to accommodate even more muck.

Albert, I thought, must think I'm green behind the ears. This place hasn't been cleaned out for two weeks at least unless it contains special horses that shit continually!

It took us all morning to clear the three stalls and spread fresh straw.

'Now, lad, after lunch—I see that you've brought a few sandwiches—we'll do a bit of winter digging.'

I was already tired out and flopped against the wall of the potting shed as Albert sat in the only chair, unscrewed his Thermos flask and began to read his paper.

I was fascinated watching Albert as he attempted to eat his meat pie whilst reading. His false teeth kept dropping on to the top of the pie as he tried to bite off a lump, but he seemed oblivious to this as his gums chased his teeth and his teeth chased the pie. Nevertheless, he somehow managed to devour the pie and still retain his teeth and was totally unaware of my amused interest.

He eventually decided lunch was over and we moved out of the shed.

'Two spits deep we're digging,' he said, handing me a spade. 'First spit in the wheelbarrow, second spit forward,' and he demonstrated. 'When barrow's full, take him to that end of plot and

134

tip him. Put plenty of manure in t' bottom of trench and then repeat the process. Got it, lad?'

'Yes, Albert,' I said, full of disinterest.

'OK, you start at that end, I'll start here,' and off we went.

The earth was light, good soil, but I was aching within five minutes.

That first day was hell; I wasn't used to manual work but my stubborn nature took me back to work next day despite the aches and pains. It soon became obvious that a pony groom, in Albert's eyes, was no more than a general labourer and I was given all the hard and dirty jobs to do while Albert fiddled in the potting shed or greenhouse.

'Albert, did you ask the boss about my bus fare?' I asked, after opening my pay packet and finding no extra money.

'You're lucky to be getting the full shop wages, son. He said he'll think about it,' said Albert. But I bet he'd never asked.

Three weeks seemed to be my limit in a job, and as the frost started in late September I stayed at home with a heavy cold. After a week I returned to Albert who sent me home again telling me he'd got someone else. Sod him, I thought, I didn't like the job anyway.

Nevertheless I was embarrassed at losing a job just then as Father was home on leave and I wasn't sure how he would take it; after all, Vic had been working ail of the time, while I'd had three jobs in the four months since leaving the Dukies. Our money was relied on to augment the family income and now I could not contribute.

'What would you like to do, Bob?' asked Father.

'Don't know, Dad.'

'Well, you'd better start thinking about it; you can't go on changing jobs every five minutes. Another thing,' he said 'I don't like you hanging around with all those ruffians on the street corner; your Mother told me about it. How would you like to join the Salvation Army? It will give you an interest.'

'Don't know, Dad. What's a Salvation Army?'

Father took me to the Army at Billericay and signed me up. They were delighted to have me but first I had to have a Bflat cornet and that was also part of Dad's great plan. He took me on the steam train to London. What an exciting day. A frosty cold sun shone on us as we walked out of Liverpool Street Station and I was so excited at the prospect of having a cornet again.

135

'It will have to be an early Christmas present, Bob.'

'Yes, Dad,' I said with excitement.

We made our way to Charing Cross Road and I gazed at beautiful, new, musical instruments in shop windows. We went into Boosey and Hawkes and Father asked if they had any secondhand Bflat cornets.

'Yes, sir, quite a selection; come this way.'

When the man mentioned the price, I got frightened that Dad might change his mind. He picked two out, both with nice, lined cases.

'Which one would you like, Bob?' I couldn't believe it.

'This one, Dad,' I said, influenced by the blue velvet lining of the carrying case.

'Would the young man like to try it in the practice room?' asked the assistant.

'No, thank you,' I said, embarrassed by all the attention.

I felt on top of the world as we walked away from the shop, me carrying my very own cornet in its beautiful carrying case.

Thursday was practice night and Sunday was playing hymns in a little church in Billericay. I enjoyed the camaraderie of the Army, was soon accepted and became a solo cornet player. But I continued to see my scruffy friends on the street corner at every opportunity.

I was always pleased when Dad was on leave and all the family were together. Dad was great around the house. He could conjure up the finest stew-pot I ever tasted. Anything and everything was put in Dad's stew. Lentils, bits of bacon, swede, parsnip, onions, meat if there was any, or "bones for the dog" if there wasn't. Any leftovers in the pantry went in, and it would simmer away all day in one of the army's big, black, iron saucepans.

We would eat our fill in the evening and Dad would top it up with more vegetables the next day, and there it was simmering when we got home again. Sometimes the pot would simmer for three days because Dad knew us older ones really appreciated his gift of making a particularly tasty stew.

One such night we'd all had our fill and were helping Dad wash up when Mum got her curling tongs out. Wetting her hair with her fingers from a bowl of water by the side of the fire, she would then put a piece of newspaper around the strands of hair and, taking the curling tongs out of the fire, pinch the bottom of the strands of hair and roll the curling tongs up to her scalp. She could carry out this dangerous operation while carrying on a conversation and looking around the room.

'Going out, Mum?' I asked with a smile.

'Just for a drink, love, with your Dad.'

I was always pleased to see Mum going out in the evening. She rarely had the opportunity and only when Dad was home.

After they had gone to The Cherry Tree for their Saturday night sing-song, I slipped out to find my friends on the street corner. They were huddled in the entrance porch of the pub out of the spitting rain.

The babble of noise wafting out into the night all but drowned the piano player thumping out *Down at the Old Bull and Bush*. It sounded so warm and cosy inside and very inviting. Occasionally the door opened as people came and went and I would peer through the thick smoke hoping to catch a glimpse of Mum. On these occasions, if she did see me, she would come outside, unbeknown to Father, and give me a giant arrowroot biscuit, sold for a penny from a glass jar on the bar, and a bottle of pop.

'Go and eat it somewhere else,' she would say with a kiss. 'Don't let your Father see you round here.'

Somewhat embarrassed at being kissed in front of the gang, I would move off with them all following. 'Give us a bit of biscuit. Give us a sip of pop.'

By the time I doled out bits of biscuit and passed the bottle round there was little left for me but it made our night. It was too cold to hang around the street corner.

'Where can we go?' asked George.

His house was always occupied by his elder brothers, the eldest being nineteen, or his baby sisters.

'My Mum and Dad are out; you can come to my house,' said Jill Murphy, and so we did.

The prefab was nice and warm and Jill had refused all but George, Alan and myself entry; the others had to go home.

Jill was a confident, show-off tom-boy who considered George her boyfriend. George had other ideas but the more he insulted her the more she clung to him.

We hadn't been in the prefab long before she coaxed George into the little kitchen. June, Alan and myself were playing cards, June with more enthusiasm than us.

'Have you got Mr Bun the Baker?' she asked Alan.

'What they doing in the kitchen?' I asked.

'Having a feel,' said Alan.

'A feel of what?' I asked.

'Oh heck,' Alan was disgusted. 'George said you don't know nuffing.'

June got annoyed. 'Mr Bun the Baker, I said. Have you got 'im?' she shouted.

'No, I haven't and I don't like this game either,' said Alan throwing his cards down. 'Let's go and join George.'

Curiosity dragged me behind them.

'Bob doesn't know what a feel is,' said Alan as George and Jill stood by the sink. 'Let him 'ave one, Jill.'

'Only if George ses so,' she replied.

What the hell are they on about? I thought.

'Can if he wants. I don't care.' replied George.

Jill advanced towards me with a mischievous smile on her face. She was wearing a faded maroon dress with high buttoned neck: a dress which had been torn and badly repaired. She was nearly as tall as me, well built but flat chested. Her round, freckled face was full of devilment.

'Go on then, have a feel and I'll feel yours.'

'Feel what? I don't know what you're talking about,' I said as laughter exploded from all three.

Jill returned to George laughing her head off as I got more annoyed.

As the laughter died down George said, 'Show 'im then.'

Jill took two paces towards me, stood astride, and lifted her frock up to her chest.

'There, what do you think of that?' she said. 'Want to feel it?'

I stared in amazement at her grubby brown knickers with a hole in the crutch.

'No, I don't. You're all dirty,' I said, going bright red. 'I'm going home.'

As I walked round the corner of Miss Outrem's shop and made my way home, I couldn't fathom why anybody would want to feel someone else's dirty brown knickers.

They must all be daft, I thought.

18

FATHER'S LAST ACT BEFORE GOING BACK off leave was to take me to see Misery Guts at the Labour Exchange again. Dressed in his uniform Dad got a lot more respect than had been given to Mum and me on previous occasions.

'"Grocery shop trainee"—should suit the boy well,' said the clerk. 'Privately owned shop, Mr and Mrs Bell are the proprietors. The vacancy only came in today.'

'Thank you,' said Dad, 'we'll go there right away.'

The grocery shop was only six hundred yards up from the Labour Exchange, on the same side of the High Street and had a stationers on one side, and a clothes shop on the other. I liked the atmosphere as soon as I walked on to the sawdust covered floor.

The shop was square, with three foot high counters, on the left and on the right, which ran the whole length of the shop. Food stuffs were neatly displayed on shelves behind them. The left-hand counter was made of grey marble and this side of the shop served bacon, margarine and butter, lard, cheese and tinned food. The wooden-topped counter on the right was dry goods. At the rear of the shop was a glass-fronted cubicle with counter; this was where the customers paid their bills and it also acted as an office.

Mrs Bell, the boss's wife, was the cashier and consequently the shop assistants worked under her constant surveillance.

Mr Bell, the boss, was about fifty years old, six feet three inches tall and as skinny as a pipe cleaner. His shoulders were rounded and his head hung in front of his body. He had a sharp-featured face that was set off by a pencil-thin pointed nose. His small eyes, like cigarette burns in a newspaper, glared out from behind his round spectacles. His hair was thinning but still black and was slicked down with hair-cream. A permanently miserable and worried expression presented a total picture of a shite-hawk that hadn't eaten for a week.

He was to prove a most difficult boss to please. His nervous

139

disposition and his habit of flitting about at speed, checking and questioning one's every action, made all of the staff thoroughly unhappy and apprehensive. Mrs Bell, who seemed to be about ten years younger than him, did her best to smooth down all the sullen animosity that her husband created.

'I'll certainly give him a fortnight's trial and see how he gets on,' Mr Bell said to Father, trying to force his face into a smile. 'He certainly looks a smart boy.'

I should do, I thought. Dad had made sure I was well scrubbed before I came out, and I was even wearing long trousers that Mum had turned up for me.

'He's a good boy and he will work hard. Thank you for giving him a chance,' said my diplomatic father.

So I started my fourth job in the second week of October 1946 and was to learn many things in the next seven months with Mr and Mrs Bell, including that peas were still on ration.

I started on the Monday morning and was kitted out in a long white coat and white apron that almost touched my shoes. Mrs Bell took charge of me that first morning and after introducing me to the five women counter assistants, I was taken to the storeroom-cum-workroom at the back of the shop.

'Do you think that you can lift that box, Robert?' she asked, pointing to one of many such boxes stacked along the wall.

'Yes, Mrs Bell,' I said, full of enthusiasm and confidence.

'Good boy, bring it into the shop then.'

Nearly breaking my back, but determined not to fail on my first task, I somehow struggled to the marble topped counter.

'Put it there,' she said. 'Now, you have a lot to learn so we must take it slowly. You won't be serving people for a while until you get used to things. I will demonstrate what I want you to do.'

She then pulled apart the top of the cardboard box to reveal a fifty-six pound block of cooking fat wrapped in greaseproof paper. We lifted it out on to a large cheese-board and Mrs Bell cut it in half with a steel wire, then into quarters.

Pushing three of the quarters out of the way, she then worked on the fourth quarter cutting it into much smaller lumps, finally using a knife to cut off match-box size pieces, one of which she placed on a small square of greaseproof paper which she then put on the scales.

'Two ounces exactly is what I want, Robert, no more and no less. Add or take off a little bit with the knife until it's exactly

140

right.' She demonstrated. 'Then it must be neatly wrapped like this,' she said, making nice square corners and tucking the points under. 'Remember the customer will weigh it when they get it home, so make sure it's right.'

So my first task started, with Mr Bell appearing at regular intervals, like a fly in a toilet, grabbing a few packets, checking their weight, and begrudgingly saying, 'All right so far,' which I came to accept as the only praise I would get.

From making up two ounce packets of cooking fat I progressed to margarine, four, six, and eight ounce packs and then occasionally, to lard in packs of one-and-a-half ounces. Lard was much easier to work with, being soft, whereas cooking fat was brittle and broke up, making it difficult to fashion into neat shapes.

For two weeks my labour of love continued with odd breaks for more menial tasks. Every night I had to sweep up all the dirty sawdust. Below this, the floor was faced with black and white composition squares, resembling a draught-board. After getting rid of the sawdust, I had to mop the floor with hot soapy suds, dry it to Mr Bell's liking and spread clean sawdust for the next day. My final job was to pull down the eight feet wide roller shutter across the entrance and padlock it and then take the key round to the side door to Mr Bell. I was always last to leave but Mrs Bell was always there to see me off the premises and often slipped me a little gift, biscuits or chocolate, when her husband wasn't looking. They lived in a flat over the shop and didn't have any children.

Beginning with my third week at the shop I was to be allowed to serve customers and Mrs Bell went over the ration book system once again.

'Buff ration book for adults and children over six years of age, green ration books for babies and small children,' she repeated. 'Adults get two ounces of cooking fat; four ounces of margarine; eight ounces of sugar; two ounces of cheese; four ounces of bacon—fat rashers as well as lean—they must have the full cut including the streaky; two ounces of tea and one shell egg if we have any. Some weeks it might change depending on what the Food Office says, so each Monday you *must* check. All right?'

'Yes, Mrs Bell.'

'Now, green ration books get three shell eggs, but only two ounces of bacon . . .' and so it went on.

How she expected me to remember all of this I don't know.

Mary was the other assistant on the marble counter and she was my immediate boss. A middle-aged woman, who had a lot of experience of rationing, she proved to be a great help to me even to the point of keeping mum about the errors I invariably made in those early days.

'How many coupons did you take for that large Shredded Wheat?' asked Mary that first day I was serving.

'Two coupons and tenpence-halfpenny,' I said.

'Three coupons, Robert,' Mary whispered. 'Two for cornflakes.' She was a good sort.

After the first month, and right out of the blue, Mrs Bell said 'Robert, Mr Bell and I are very pleased with your progress and hard work. You will be getting seven-and-sixpence a week rise from today.'

'Thank you, Mrs Bell,' was all I said although I could have shouted for joy. Wait till I get home and tell them all, I loved the work and the job; life at last seems to be settling into a pattern, I thought.

As I walked up Britannia Road that Monday evening in the November wind and rain I was feeling proud and happy. My first rise. I don't think it was just the extra money which lifted my spirits, more a sense of being recognised. 'Very pleased with your progress and hard work,' she had said. I didn't think they'd noticed me. It was a great feeling being recognised as a valuable and hard-working person. I burst through the front door, through the passage and into the living-room.

'Mum, I got a rise; Mrs Bell said I'm a hard worker.'

'That's nice, Bobby,' said Mum, rolling the milk bottle over the pastry. 'It's only what you deserve,' she said, flouring the bottle.

I don't think I ever saw or knew of a rolling pin until I was eighteen years old. Pauline was at Mum's elbow helping as usual.

'Mum, I've saved some money. Can I have a real suit?' I asked.

'We don't have enough clothing coupons, love; we'll get you one soon.'

The issue of clothing coupons seemed to be worked out by some genius in the government so that few people had enough for even basic necessities . . . unless you had money, that is. There was a thriving black market in them, forged, stolen—and even pawned. I knew "Uncle's" was in on the game. I think Mum had reason to know it too, so I didn't persist.

Vic was home that day, sitting by the fire and waiting for tea. He often worked on the building site on Sundays, which paid double time, and he would then take Monday off.

'You only pay it back in tax if you work all the time,' he would say.

He heard the conversation with Mum and said, 'I'll take you to Petticoat Lane on Sunday morning; you don't need coupons there.'

'Thanks,' I said full of excitement and picturing my first new suit, but Mum was worried.

'Oh, I don't know, Vic. It could be dangerous, you two with all those Londoners. Why don't you wait till your Dad comes home?'

'It'll be all right,' said Vic. 'We'll be careful.'

Early Sunday morning we caught the Greenline bus to Aldgate East, about an hour's ride, and got off almost opposite the tube station. A weak winter sun was trying to warm us on that dry but frosty morning.

We crossed the road and walked the fifty yards to Middlesex Street, better known as Petticoat Lane, famous for selling anything and everything in those early years after the war.

'How much money have you got?' asked Vic.

'Nine pounds twelve shillings,' I said. The fruits of my working life.

'Well, keep your hand in your pocket and stay close to me,' said Vic. 'Don't show all your money; have a few bob in a separate pocket to buy any little things.'

'Okay,' I replied.

The market stalls seemed to stretch for miles, from Aldgate to Liverpool Street Station. Most of the stallholders were Jews and the area had taken its fair share of bombs, with large gaps where buildings had been razed to the ground. The street was a sea of people pushing and shoving in all directions. The cries of the cockney stallholders echoed over our heads and I thought how happy and musical some of them sounded. My dear old friends, the Sally Army, were trying to be heard as they belted out a hymn on the first bomb site, right opposite a woman gutting chickens on a stall outside a pub, The Unicorn, I think.

Vic ploughed on through the crush; I clutched my money and kept close. Most of the stalls had crowds around them listening to the patter of the cockney salesmen. Vic pushed his way through to the front of a couple of stalls and I was fascinated with the patter and with the variety of goods on sale. I even saw my first bananas but I didn't dare ask how much they cost!

Eventually we found the clothes stalls. They were just off the

143

street in an old Victorian building. Every type of suit, overcoat, jacket and trousers was on sale. I couldn't believe our luck.

'Sure, son, I've got summat that 'ul fit you,' said the well-fed owner, as he took a suit from the rack. 'You're a bit skinny but you'll grow into this,' he said, proffering a brown jacket with a fine maroon strip in the cloth. The suit was lovely; it was double-breasted, wide collar and the trousers had a one inch turn-up.

'Try the jacket,' said Vic.

It was a bit big but I was thrilled to have it on, absolutely thrilled. 'Mum can move the buttons over,' Vic said.

'That's real fashion, son,' said the salesman. 'Just feel the quality.'

'How much is it?' asked Vic.

'Twenty-five quid, mate,' he replied.

I nearly died with disappointment.

'We've only got nine pound twelve,' said Vic.

'You're wasting my time, son; go save your coupons; I couldn't flog you the jacket for that.'

We walked away and I bit my lip to stop the tears of disappointment. Twenty-five pounds was a fortune. I'd never get a suit, I thought.

We went for a cup of tea and wandered around the stalls for another hour. I felt devastated. I'd built up my hopes so high.

Escape artists were working on a crowd that had gathered on a bombsite behind the rows of stalls. 'Learnt his trade from the famous Houdini,' the spieler was shouting. 'Been all over the world. Today he's trying out something for the very first time; and if it goes wrong it's curtains. Come along now, show your generosity,' as two assistants carried round a stretched-out Union Jack with coins already on it.

'First it's the strait-jacket,' continued the spieler. 'Check it if you like, real leather straps and metal buckles.' The escape artist was being fitted up and making a big show about it. 'Next it's the chains and padlocks. Can I have someone from the audience to examine the padlocks.'

All good patter, well drawn out to maximise the take. And so it went on, milking every coin from the increasing crowd.

'Now you see him for the last time before he goes in the crate. The crate will then be lifted by the crane and he 'as one minute's wurf of air 'ermetically sealed in the crate before it's curtains. What an 'ell of a way to earn a living! Come on, give generously.

144

We gets more at a church fair.'

More time was wasted checking the padlocks on the crate and then it was raised in the air. The crowd hushed. I felt quite excited. How could he possibly get out of a straight-jacket, masses of chains and a padlocked crate while swinging ten feet in the air?

'Start counting. He's only got sixty seconds to live.'

The crowd were slow to start but, after thirty, most were joining in. The crate was swaying above our heads. Fifty-one, fifty-two, fifty-three—great excitement. At fifty-eight, as by a miracle, the crate top burst open; no-one noticed it opened from the hinged side. The escape artist dangled by one arm as the crane lowered him to the ground. Applause all round as the crowd started to disperse, a few people not yet aware that they were short of their purses or wallets. An hour had passed.

'Look, Vic, saucepans,' I said as we continued to wander around the stalls. Many a time I'd heard Mum say to Dad how she wished she had some real modern saucepans.

'You can't get 'em, Vi,' Fred used to say.. 'They're not making them yet.' So Mother continued to struggle with the big, black, iron army saucepans with their great tubular handles which it took two hands to lift.

'Do you think we can buy some for Mum's Christmas present?'

'Let's see what they cost first,' said Vic, so we stood and watched.

'Made from a Jerry bomber,' the man shouted. 'Finest aluminium that 'itler could produce. I'm not asking twenty quid, not even ten. Go on then, the first five hands up for a set of four saucepans. I must be crackers, five pounds ten.'

I looked at Vic all excited. 'Let's get 'um, Vic, quick, before they're all gone,' and so we made our purchase. They were packed in a nice box and we set off home as happy as could be.

Looking back I have many family memories to cherish but the one I hold dearest is the expression of delight on Mum's face when she opened her parcel that Christmas morning. I don't think there was anything in the world that a millionaire could have bought that could have pleased her more. She was ecstatic and as always, when she was happy, she cried.

Over the years I bought Mother many presents, some quite expensive, but none of them ever evoked the same total response.

None.

19

I STILL PLAYED THE CORNET with the Sally Army twice a
week and now Christmas was approaching extra engagements were
taken on. I often found myself playing outside Woollies or the Co-
op as snowflakes settled all over us. I was getting good at snooker
too and took George along sometimes to the snooker hall above
Burtons.

Going to the pictures was a weekly ritual, usually on a
Wednesday which was the shop's half day closing as we worked all
day Saturday. That was the only thing I didn't like about shop
work as all my friends were free on Saturday afternoons.

'Come with me, Robert,' said Mr Bell. I think you're ready to
learn how to skin a cheese.'

The back storeroom of the shop was twenty feet square. Fats,
cheeses and bacon were stored on one side of the concrete floor
and dried goods and canned food on the opposite side. The third
side had a square, vitreous clay sink, a gas ring and a round, grey
copper. The entrance door was in the fourth side with a sash
window to the right of it. In the centre of the floor stood a hefty
workbench, eight feet long and three feet wide, not unlike a big
butcher's block.

'Right, Robert, let's get these two cheeses into the middle of the
floor.'

The cheeses, two of them, were stacked one above the other in
a round, wooden, slatted crate. They were eighteen inches in
diameter and one foot deep. Each slat of the crate had a steel wire
stapled along its length which ran from beneath the crate right
through to the top. The gaps between the slats allowed the cheese
to breathe and the steel wire ensured that even with rough
handling, the heavy cheeses didn't break out of the crate.

'Right,' said Mr Bell. 'First we take the pliers and cut through
the steel wire on each slat. Then draw out the staples with the

146

pliers,' he said, as he demonstrated. 'Now we knock out the top of the crate with the hammer and break off the top of the slats. Good,' he said, praising himself and staring at the exposed round uppermost cheese, while the one below was still trapped in its prison.

'Now fetch the big tin bath from the yard, stand it by the bench and fill it with hot water from the copper. It's boiling,' he said. 'so be careful. About two thirds will do and I'll be back in a minute.' And off he went.

'Right, Robert,' he said on returning. 'We now gently lower the cheese into hot water; it's heavy, so watch it.'

We took a side each of the awkward shape and gingerly lowered it into the steamy water which lapped over the bath edge on to the stone floor.

'Now it soaks for five minutes. You might as well have your tea-break now.'

'Thank you, Mr Bell.'

This is interesting, I thought. I like this sort of job. Hope he lets me do one myself next time.

'It should be well soaked now,' he said on my return. 'Let's get it on to the bench and be careful. It's very slippery.'

Once on the bench we proceeded to peel off a number of layers of white cheese-cloth. This cheese-cloth is used to cover the inside of the cheese-maker's mould before he pours the liquid cheese in. The top of the cheese is also covered with the same material as it is setting. When the cheese is set it is then easy to extract from its mould as the cheese-cloth acts like grease in a cake tin and provides a skin which protects the cheese until it is required.

So I learnt how to skin my first cheese. When all the cloth had been removed, Mr Bell positioned the cheese on the bench where the cutting wire hung.

'Watch, Robert,' he said, as he grasped the wooden toggle at the end of the wire. 'Make sure you have positioned the wire in the centre of the cheese; then pull down firmly but slowly. There, the cheese is halved.' As he parted the two halves the smell was gorgeous; I'll always remember that smell.

'Now we take one half and cut it into quarters and then eighths. The other half must be covered in a wet sack and laid face down on the floor until it is required. That's good, Robert. Do you think you can do that now?'

'Oh yes, Mr Bell.'

'Good, but it's a two man job lifting it in and out of the bath; you can try the next one when we need it.'

Feeling more important than ever I started to clean up the mess and get my newly-cut cheese into the shop. It was a lovely job skinning cheeses and what a lovely taste to pop a fresh lump into your mouth when no-one was looking. Mr Bell seemed to have got over the telling-off he had given me the week before. I had thought I was going to get the sack.

'Robert,' he'd said, appearing from nowhere like a genie out of a lamp. 'How many coupons did you take for that tin of peas?'

'None, Mr Bell,' I said. Peas aren't on ration. Mr Doe next door grows them in his garden.'

He went berserk: the whole shop stopped serving. Counter assistants and customers alike were all looking at us.

'You stupid boy, how long have you been doing this? And what about the tinned carrots and beans?' Before I could reply Mrs Bell rescued the situation.

'John, let's go out the back and discuss it,' and I believed that Mr Bell only then realised where he was and that all the customers were listening.

We all trooped out the back to much whispering and sympathetic glances towards me. I didn't get the sack thanks to Mrs Bell who seemed to be my guardian angel.

As we moved into December I was really getting on well. I knew all the customers and coupon values and was gathering a gaggle of regulars at my position on the counter who seemed to like me serving them.

Mrs Vernon was my favourite old lady because she was like my Grandma. A short lady, maybe five feet four, with a nice round soft face, a quiet and polite voice and appreciative, warm eyes. Her silver grey hair was always drawn into a neat bun on the back of her head and she was immaculately dressed. Since her husband's death early in the war, she had run her gents' outfitters shop opposite the White Hart Hotel in the High Street. She always came to me to be served; Mary didn't mind. She had her regulars anyway. I felt sorry for Mrs Vernon; having only one ration book made her order look pitiful.

'Hello, Robert,' she'd say. 'What a cold day. You must be freezing behind there with the wind coming through the big door.'

'I am, Mrs Vernon, but we have a heater at the end of the counter so I go down there for a warm when nobody's in.'

Always so considerate of others, I thought. What a lovely lady. I always made sure she had no bits of fat in her bacon ration; in fact, I changed some of the streaky for short back and hid it under a slice of streaky on top.

'I have two broken eggs if you'd like them, Mrs Vernon.'

'Oh, thank you, Robert.' She beamed more thanks through her eyes.

Often eggs got broken in transit and got stuck to the egg cartons. We were supposed to offer these "under the counter" eggs to regular customers with lots of ration books. Mr Bell had gone away again for a couple of days to see his ailing mother in Kent. Mrs Bell was left in charge, so I felt safe in offering extras to my favourite customer.

She handed me a lidded container that she now carried in the hope I'd have a broken egg. In fact I'd saved these two all week for her and, on occasion, broke one on purpose when no-one was looking. I couldn't have her going away without at least one broken egg.

'Mrs Vernon,' I whispered. 'Would you like a Heinz Salad Cream?' What a stupid question, I thought. Most people would give their right arm for a bottle. Just two cartons had arrived last week and Mr Bell had given strict instructions.

'Customers with three books or more only. Wait until they are on their own or get them to the end of the counter. Never show it openly; put it in a bag before you raise it above the counter,' and so it went on. HP Sauce, ketchup, pickle, salad cream and, later on, the very first custard cream biscuits, were all destined to hide in the dark, under the counter, only to come out for the favoured few. Well, I thought, Mrs Vernon deserved it.

'Oh, please, Robert, yes, please. I can't remember when I last had any.' In the paper bag it went and then to grateful hands; it was secreted with care into her basket. I did feel good helping Mrs Vernon; it was like helping my Gran, Father's mother, who was such a gracious lady.

Towards Christmas the shop was very busy. There was great excitement amongst the staff as one morning, before we opened the shutter door, Mr Bell read out the list of extra goods that had arrived. He repeated his instructions on the *modus operandi* for under the counter goods. 'Custard creams will be made up in quarter pound bags.'

All biscuits came in large tins and were sold loose: no packet biscuits. Wonder upon wonder, I thought, long boxes of dates arrived with colourful pictures of camels and palm trees. I'd pluck up courage and ask Mr Bell if I could have a box.

'To qualify for one box of dates the customer must have a minimum of three ration books, one of which must be a green one,' he told me.

'Bugger me,' whispered Alice, a dry goods assistant. 'He don't 'arf make it difficult! First come, first served, I'd say,' and knowing nods were returned by the others.

A large taped box with a slot in it was placed on each counter by Mr Bell. A notice announced "Staff Gratuities".

'All tips will be put in the boxes and shared out on Christmas Eve,' declared the boss.

Fair enough, I thought.

Mrs Vernon came in for her Christmas week's rations. I'd secreted under my marble counter a quarter pound of custard creams from dry goods, with the knowledge of the counter staff. I slipped them to her when the boss wasn't looking.

When Mrs Vernon had completed her purchases she came across to me and with a smiling face offered me a brand new, white, five pound note, saying 'Happy Christmas, Robert.' I was flabbergasted.

'Oh, I couldn't take that, Mrs Vernon; that's a lot of money. Anyway it has to go in the box.'

'No, Robert, this is my present to you,' she said.

'I'm sorry, Mrs Vernon; I'm not allowed to take it.'

'We'll see about that,' she said in a much more commanding voice than I'd heard before. She strode the three steps to the kiosk where the Bells were in conversation.

'I'm sure you'd have no objection if I gave Robert a private gift for Christmas,' she said, showing the beautiful fiver.

'We have a rule, Mrs Vernon; share and share alike. All gifts must go in the boxes and be shared,' Mr Bell told her.

'Poppycock,' said Mrs Vernon, striding out of the shop.

I looked down at my feet feeling embarrassed; I couldn't meet anyone's eye. That's the quickest fiver I'd ever had and lost, I thought. I continued to weigh and package the cheese.

To my great surprise, just ten minutes later, back came Mrs Vernon; straight up to Mr Bell she went. Drawing her hand from her bag she displayed a beautiful, hand-woven, Fair Isle tie.

'You won't be able to put this in the box and share it out, will you?' With that she walked over and gave it to me. 'Happy Christmas, Robert,' she said as her eyes twinkled.

I do believe she got great enjoyment from that encounter, and I treasured that tie for many years and always wore it on Thursdays, Mrs Vernon's ration day.

We had a smashing Christmas that year. Mrs Bell had helped by giving me a large cardboard box full of most commodities in the shop, including a box of dates. I don't know whether the rest of the staff got the same as I did; I doubt it. It would have emptied the shelves.

Mrs Bell often had long talks with me, so she knew all about the family, my life history, India and the Dukies.

'Poor Robert,' she would say. 'You haven't had much home life or loving have you?'

Dad brought home quite a lot of food too, including a huge tin of cooking fat, tinned fish and even a tin of cheese. For once we had more than enough to eat.

Father was a great host as usual. Striding around the kitchen in his long white apron, while Mum was preparing the bird for Christmas dinner. The turkey had appeared with the cooking fat, fish and cheese, compliments of the army cookhouse, I expect. Father stuffed the bird with his home-made stuffing. He would toast slices of bread and break it into crumbs with a milk bottle, add water, chopped onions and parsley, thyme and a little salt; then he would stuff it in the turkey with enthusiasm as he hummed a tune.

That Christmas was the first time I ever had whisky in my tea. Father, always an early riser, had woken us up with a cheery smile and brought up a tray bearing steaming hot mugs of tea.

'Tastes funny, Dad,' I said after the first sip.

'Whisky Bob, that's the way to start Christmas Day; keeps the cold out, too.'

From then on it became a Freeman ritual on Christmas mornings. Many years later, when Dad was a Chelsea Pensioner, it was Christmas every day as he put a drop of whisky in every cup of tea.

Dad liked a show, he loved surprising us. I have vivid memories of us all sitting round the table. The plates from the main course had been cleared and we awaited Dad's entry from the

151

kitchen with the Christmas pud. He never took off his white apron or his party hat, even to eat, and his apron nearly reached the floor.

Mum and the five of us sat waiting expectantly. In burst Father, face beaming as he carried in the steaming black Christmas pudding with a sprig of red-berried holly sticking out of the top.

'Da-darm'—Dad would make a noise like a drum roll. With a flourish and great panache, as though he had an audience of a thousand people, he would uncap the whisky bottle and pour a liberal measure over the pud. Bottle capped and put away, he then struck a match. With a small woof the pudding burst into flames.

There were expressions of amazement and smiles all around until Mum said, 'Fred, you've caught the decorations.'

Sure enough, the low-hung paper chains and streamers were burning nicely and for one panicky moment we spontaneously moved from the table.

Father with great calm and one quick pull, had the blazing decorations out through the sash window into the yard in a second. Panic over, we all laughed. Yet what really made Christmas that year was the joy of seeing Mum open her present of saucepans.

Dad was still on leave on New Year's Eve, my first New Year at home. 'You can stay up and see New Year in if you like, Bob,' said Father after tea.

'Thanks, Dad,' I said, not really knowing what he meant.

We were all sitting in the cosy warm back room, with the fire roaring in the black grate. Those Christmas decorations which had survived were still up and all the family sat in a semi-circle round the grate listening to a special edition of Itma with Tommy Handley. At nine o'clock Mother put Pauline and Roger to bed, Pauline protesting that she was nearly as old as Ernie, but Father's decision saw his daughter sulk off "up the wooden hill."

Dad fetched a stone flagon of Bulmer's cider from The Cherry Tree and we played cards sitting round the square white pinewood table. Dad was good at cards and knew every game; his favourite was crib and he knew every call. 'Twenty-four, sevens no more,' he would call as he laid his card. 'Twenty-six, fives are fixed,' or 'twenty-nine, twos in time for four.' He could count up a hand quicker than any of us.

Mum was listening to the wireless as the four of us played cards. She was unravelling an old sweater and winding the wool into balls ready for the next knitting session. Her hands were never idle, either patching or repairing our clothes, knitting, knitting,

152

knitting, or making peg rugs for the house. These colourful rugs were upstairs in the bedrooms and in both rooms downstairs. It's marvellous what can be made from strips of coloured cloth cut from old clothes and a bit of sacking.

'Shush, shush,' said Mum. 'Big Ben's going to strike, get the coal and wood, Vic.'

We all pulled our upright chairs back round the fire and Big Ben struck the first stroke of midnight. The wireless returned to its audience who were singing Auld Lang Syne and we joined in. Mum put out her hands to us and we all linked up; she was beaming as tears poured down her face. My first real New Year at home and all the family were together.

Auld Lang Syne finished and Vic dashed out the back door, ran like a hare round the terraced block and knocked on the front door. Dad let him in, accepting the lump of coal and piece of kindling.

'May you all have a happy and warm New Year,' said Vic. It certainly started that way as Father brewed his special blend of "sergeant major's tea," laced with whisky.

So I'm glad I didn't know what the future held for me: that this would be the first and last New Year together for a long time. Life has a strange way of dealing out the cards and my hand—not for the first time—was going to be a poor one.

20

I WAS NOW BECOMING QUITE PROFICIENT at most aspects of the grocery business and, in the New Year, Mr Bell taught me how to bone a side of bacon.

'Make sure the knife is really sharp,' he would say, having a private duel with the knife and the sharpening steel. 'Each rib must come out clean; I don't want to see any bacon on it at all.' He deftly demonstrated the technique. After a few attempts I got the hang of it.

'Now, cutting the side into portions is very important; they must be square or we get waste on the slicing machine, and cut right down to the knuckle for the first cut and work upwards.'

I soon got the hang of that, too. Sometimes, by accident, a knuckle had much more bacon left on it than it should have had, and I had to take it home so that Mr Bell wouldn't see it and make a fuss.

We had a foot of snow in the New Year and once it started snowing it didn't seem to want to stop. I was in a foul mood, standing on the wide pavement outside the shop. My feet were like blocks of ice and I'd even had to change the cardboard inside my shoes because it got soaking wet while I was snow clearing. My hands were freezing and my fingers were like thin, white candles. The snow was falling as fast as I was shovelling. I thought, What's the use? The boss was in a foul mood too, as were the staff.

The BBC and the newspapers kept repeating the Government warnings: "Energy Crisis", "Coal Shortage", "If customers don't reduce consumption of gas and electricity by 25% from last year's usage, power cuts will take place in many areas".

Mr Bell had taken the message to heart and was determined to save the whole country. 'All heaters will be switched off permanently,' he decreed.

The door to the shop was an eight feet wide roller shutter we had to leave up, and with snow being blown into the shop, it was like working in a cold store. We had put up with it for a week now and I was getting fed up. None of the ladies had complained to the boss, only to each other.

'It's no use you leaving those lumps of ice there, Robert. That's what the shovel's for; chip them off,' said Mr Bell always checking, always criticising, never encouraging.

The footprints where people had walked had melted and then frozen again on to the pavement. Like shit on a blanket, they wouldn't come off.

The black and white rubber floor in the shop only extended as far as the counters. Behind them we stood on bare concrete, from which cold struck through to our very bones.

The rebellious streak that was always just below the surface was rising again within me and ready to erupt. I put my broom and shovel away and joined Mary who was packing margarine. She was stamping her feet and blowing on her hands. I couldn't fold the greaseproof round the four ounce blocks of margarine because my fingers were frozen.

Sod this, I thought, and on impulse I walked up to Mr Bell by the kiosk and said in a loud voice:

'I'm not working unless I can have the heater on. I'm freezing.'

The whole shop went quiet; fortunately there were no customers in. Mr Bell's jaw dropped; he was taken aback by this unexpected frontal attack. His eyes narrowed to pin-points, like pee holes in snow.

'It's the same for everybody. Nobody else is complaining; now get back to your work.'

I was nervous, frightened even, but as in all these situations I became obstinate. My true self was surfacing. If it didn't seem fair or logical, I could never accept the situation.

'No, I'm not working without the heater; we're all frozen,' I said.

I knew what was coming. I was about to tell him where to stick his job when Mrs Bell stepped in.

'Come out the back and let's talk about it,' she said.

Trembling a bit with emotion I followed them both out to the store-room.

'John, get one of the girls to make some tea, will you? I'll speak to Robert. Make it for all the staff, John,' she said.

'Speak with him if you like, Janet, but there will be no heaters

155

on in this shop, and that's final,'

I would do anything for Mrs Bell; she had always been very kind to me, more like a second mother. She gave me things and made a fuss of me and sometimes it was embarrassing being made a fuss of in front of the staff. She would often say, 'Have you got a girlfriend, Robert?' and I would blush.

'No,' was my reply.

'I know you must be cold,' she was saying. 'We're all cold; I'm cold in my kiosk without my heater on.'

'But the cold gets right into my bones standing on that cold concrete, Mrs Bell.'

The tea came in and Mary gave me a smile of solidarity.

'Haven't you got some thicker socks at home and maybe another pullover?' she asked. 'You really mustn't get upset like this; promise me you won't make a scene in the shop again. If you have something worrying you, come and tell me in the kiosk; I'm sure we'll sort it out. Now I'll tell you what we will do,' she continued. 'I'll get some strips of carpet for behind both counters. That will help, won't it?' she said, smiling. And we will have an extra break in the morning and afternoon for a mug of Oxo; how does that sound?'

I had calmed down by then and we sat on two rickety chairs by the workbench, Mrs Bell finishing off her cup of tea.

'All right, Mrs Bell, if you say so, thank you.'

'There's a good boy,' she said, patting my cheek. 'You stay and finish your tea; come through when you are ready.'

The second-hand carpet came and hot Oxo was enjoyed by all except Mr Bell, who took a dislike to me. Fortunately a week later he went to see his ailing mother again and no doubt stocked her pantry with groceries.

The second day he was away we were getting low on cheese. Mrs Bell didn't tear about checking up on everything and everybody like her husband did, but it didn't seem to make any difference. I'd spotted it anyway. I'll skin a cheese after lunch, I thought. That will keep me warm with the copper boiling and working with the hot water.

I went off at one o'clock to Harry's café, forty yards down the High Street. It was cheap and tatty, but warm and friendly. He was an ex-army chap running his own one-man business and doing quite nicely by all accounts.

'Beans on toast, Harry, and tea, please,' I said, giving my order.

156

'You'll look like a baked bean soon,' he quipped.

'Brought up on them,' I told him. 'Good old cavalry stand-by.'

He was a friendly guy to all his customers, regulars or not. I went over to the pintable machine to try my luck. One penny in the slot, score a hundred thousand or over and claim sixpence off Harry. I wasted tuppence without even getting a Tilt which was some achievement on that old battered and abused machine.

'Beans on toast,' called Harry.

I ate my lunch slowly, watching the other customers and ear-wigging on conversations. Why was it that women were always talking about men, and men, when together, were always talking about women? Was there nothing else in the world worth talking about? I thought, as I walked back to the shop.

I soon had the copper boiling and the cheese soaking in the tin bath. I made myself an Oxo and sipped it while the cheese was soaking. Thank God Hawkeye's not here, I thought as I surveyed the wet floor. He did tell me only to fill the bath two thirds full. I'd caused a great wave when I'd dropped the cheese in the water and now the floor was swimming. I'd mop up when I finished, I thought.

I let the cheese soak for five minutes and finished the Oxo. Then I bent over the bath, sleeves rolled up, and up to my elbows in water. I took a grip on the slippery cheese.

I was in my own dream world, miles away, when, just behind me, someone spoke. It was totally unexpected. The shock made me jump. The cheese went one way and I went the other.

'There you are, Robert,' said Mrs Bell, 'I thought you had gone out to lunch.'

But before she had got all the words out the slippery cheese had been propelled like a projectile back into the water. A great wave shot up the side of the bath and soaked me from head to toe. I stood there drenched, water everywhere.

'Are you all right Robert?' asked Mrs Bell anxiously.

'Yes . . . I'm OK,' I said, wiping the water from my eyes.

'Come upstairs quickly and I'll get you dried out,' she said.

'No, it's all right, Mrs Bell. I'll go home.'

'You certainly will not in that state, Robert. This way,' she said.

I reluctantly followed her up the private stairs into a well carpeted and furnished lounge. She went quickly across the room and through another door.

I stood dripping on the lovely, patterned carpet, looking around at the posh furniture, beautiful sofa and two matching chairs. An expensive modern gas fire was set in the wall. A highly polished dining table and four matching chairs glowed by the window and a corner cabinet, brimming with best china, had a silver teapot setting off the display. A glass-fronted bookcase filled with books, including a matching set with gold titling, stood at the side of the fire, and a healthy green leafed plant filled a corner by long curtains framing a large window overlooking the High Street. Half a dozen framed photographs hung on the walls. The room looked luxurious yet cosy, quite the nicest room I'd ever seen.

'Don't stand there, Robert; go into the bathroom and get those wet clothes off,' she said. 'I've run the bath so you can have a good soak. It's going to take me at least twenty minutes to iron and air your trousers.'

Have a bath in this strange flat; no thank you, I thought, frightened at the idea. I hesitated, not knowing what to do and suddenly she had hold of my arm.

'Come along, Robert, you're dripping all over my carpet.' She led me across the lounge, through the bedroom and into the bathroom. 'Take your clothes off and get into that lovely warm bath. I'll collect the clothes shortly,' she said, and disappeared.

I stood for a moment confused and trembly. The bathroom was lovely, all pinks and greys. There were nice tiles on the wall around the bath. A full length mirror was fixed on the back of the door. The bath was boxed in; you couldn't see the legs. There was a gleaming white hand basin and toilet too. A big bath towel hung next to a smaller hand towel, neatly folded on a wall bar. There was a fluffy bathmat alongside the bath, and soap, talcum powder and various white pots neatly displayed on a shelf, even toilet paper on a roll.

That's a novelty—better than newspaper squares, I thought.

At home, we usually had a bath on a Friday. I generally followed Vic, sometimes Mum, but I always warmed the water up with an extra kettle. Up until then, I don't remember ever being the first to get into a fresh bath. Even in the Dukies it was two at a time in eight inches of water. So here I stood, in a fantastic bathroom, with a bath two-thirds full of steaming, scented fresh water. Mrs Bell must have put something in it to make millions of bubbles; it did smell nice and inviting.

I listened at the door, no sound at all, so I took my courage in both hands and disrobed in seconds. Into the warm bubbly water I went; what luxury, sheer bliss. I sank up to my chin and from being in cold, wet clothes I was now wrapped in a perfumed, warm blanket. With my eyes closed, the beautiful smell and the warm soft water seemed to lift me up on a cloud, floating, floating, just like Sabu on his magic carpet, flying over the mosques, palaces and bazaars of Baghdad, the last picture I'd seen at the Odeon.

'You're enjoying that, Robert, I can see.'

Startled, I came to; Mrs Bell was standing there looking down at me. I went beetroot red. Thank God for the bubbles, I thought. She can't see me.

'I'll soon have your clothes ironed and aired,' she said as she scooped them all up and disappeared.

I calmed down again and started to wash myself with her scented soap. Better than Lifebuoy , I thought. I hated that smell.

The water was getting cooler and what was worse, the bubbles were rapidly disappearing. Panic set in; I splashed the water about but no more bubbles came; in fact it seemed to make the few remaining ones disappear. I could see the whole length of my white body. Oh, Christ, what could I do?

Mrs Bell was there again. 'Come on, Robert, let's have you out; your clothes will be aired in a few minutes,' she said as she pulled out the plug by its chain.

I was struck dumb, terrified, couldn't move. I expected her to bring my clothes back and disappear, yet here she was, pulling the big towel off the wall and she was saying, 'I'll help you to get dried.'

She could see all of me; I sat there, as the last of the water gurgled away. A million thoughts were racing through my confused mind. Since I joined the Dukies not even my Mum had seen me without any clothes on.

'Stand up, Robert. I can't dry you down there. Don't be shy.'

She was tugging at my shoulders. As she bent over me I smelt her perfume. She had taken off her white shop coat and her breasts flopped forward in her loose blouse. I was burning up. My face was flaming. Should I run and try and find my clothes? Should I scream? But no-one would hear me. For some daft reason I thought of Jill Murphy's brown, flannelette knickers. I was on my feet, and her hands were all over me.

'That's better; now I can dry you properly,' she said.

Why had her eyes gone funny? I thought. I stood there, on the

159

little mat by the bath.   I could see Mrs Bell's legs reflected in the full length mirror on the back of the door; I had never really noticed them, or her small bum, before.

'Lift your arms up,' she said and, mechanically I obeyed.

I was hypnotised. She was saying something again but I was in Warley Barracks wood with George and Alan watching a soldier doing it. The towel and hands were drying my private parts. Hell, what was happening? I felt a tingling, hot feeling creeping over my groin. She bent down to dry my legs and ankles and I saw it.

My thing was three times as big as normal and sticking out like a chapel hat peg.

I went rigid, rooted to the spot, as though struck by lightning, like a horse peeing in a field with his back legs braced. She was looking up at me, smiling.

'It's nothing to be ashamed of Robert; you're a man now.' She put her soft hand on it and stroked it gently; she was still on her knees and her eyes were not four inches away. I couldn't move; the embarrassment was confused with the utter pleasure of what was happening. Her touch became more urgent. My first awakening, never to be forgotten.

"Bang," the bullet hit the mirror three feet away. As my body convulsed like an earthquake into a flood of tears and sobbing, the chapel hat peg miraculously changed into a boiled snail as it swiftly shrank back into its shell.   Mrs Bell had me clutched between her breasts. My crying, from embarrassment and a new experience, was soaking her blouse.

'There, there, Robert, nothing to cry about; you're a healthy young man; this happens to everybody,' she said. 'Dry your tears now and I'll make a pot of tea. I've a lovely cake for you. Come on, stop crying and get dressed; your clothes will be aired by now.'

As she clutched me to her, those soft hands were stroking my bum. Her voice seemed husky and I was nearly smothered as she clutched me tightly.

'Let's keep this our secret, Robert; no-one needs to know, do they?'

'No, Mrs Bell,' I croaked for the first time. I'm certainly not going to tell anyone about this, I thought.

I don't remember the journey home. I was ashamed of what had happened and totally confused. I was only sure of one thing; I wasn't going back to the shop, ever; no way could I face or look at Mrs Bell again.

I was hoping everyone would be out as I walked up Britannia Road but they weren't. 'Your tea's in the oven, Bobby,' Mum sang out. 'We've had ours.'

'I'm not hungry, Mum; I don't want any,' I replied.

Mum came out of the kitchen, full of motherly concern and took my head in her hands and looked at me. I'd never refused my food before and she knew something was wrong.

'You look pale, darling. Are you sickening for something?' she asked, as if I could answer. I burst into tears again; my day for tears it seemed. 'I don't want to work at the shop any more, Mum,' I blurted out.

'There, love, you've no need to get upset. Had another row with Mr Bell, have you? Don't fret, love; go to bed and I'll bring you a warm drink.'

Mother never questioned why I'd left the shop; she may have thought she knew, but I knew different. She agreed to call in and tell Mr and Mrs Bell I wasn't coming back. What they said I don't know but I can guess Mr Bell would think, 'Good riddance,' and Mrs Bell would keep her secret. They sent me a generous amount of money, more than I was entitled to, and I guess Mrs Bell was responsible for that.

Looking back in later years I often wonder what would have happened if I'd continued working there. Something would have happened, and that's for sure, but we can all look back and play the game of "If only." It means nothing.

That's the way it was and life moved on.

21

BACK TO MISERY GUTS and a few sarcastic words at the Labour Exchange; two days later I was working in a damp, draughty barn at the bottom of Brook Street Hill. The job was unscrewing ammunition boxes on piecework. Every screw, nail, metal corner piece and webbing strap handle had to be removed. The salvaged wood was then sliced up into four inch planks with a powered ripsaw. We stacked our salvaged wood in separate piles so that the number of pieces could be recorded. If the machine hit a nail or screw in one of your planks you were deducted at least half an hour's pay, more if the saw blade was damaged.

I stood in line with the other labourers and worked as fast as I could. Some of the men were stripping four boxes to my one. The foreman blew a whistle for a ten minute morning break but there was no break in the afternoon.

After the first day my hands were cut, sore and ingrained with dirt. On top of that I was tired out. I kept thinking, Why did I drop that bloody cheese? If only I had got someone to help with the lifting like I was told to by Mr Bell. If, if, if. I missed Harry's café too, a bit different to sitting in a cold shed with sandwiches and a Thermos flask. Somehow I managed to stagger through the first week and I was dumbfounded to see my wages were only just above half what I'd been getting in the shop.

The foreman had noticed my poor performance and on Monday he said, 'Would you like to try seed-boxes? It's still piecework but easier on the hands.'

'Yes, please,' I said, grasping at straws. Anything to get away from pulling those bloody awful ammunition boxes apart. He took me to another barn type building across a quagmire of mud and rubble. The noise was deafening as we approached and ten times worse as we entered.

A row of twelve robots stood spaced out along a bench against

162

the far wall, hammering away like mad. From the ready cut lengths of timber I'd been preparing, eleven women and one man were fashioning four inch deep seed boxes. Ammunition boxes became seed boxes, the sword to the ploughshare; how true. One woman, in apron and headscarf, looked as if she was eighteen months pregnant. I knew where she'd been and blushed at the thought. I hoped he didn't put me next to her.

'Jenny left last week; you can take her place,' bellowed the foreman with his mouth inside my ear. He pointed to the far end of the barn.

'Molly will show you the ropes; she's the chargehand and not on piecework,' he shouted.

Molly had me nailing the boxes together in no time. We weren't happy; we couldn't talk because of the noise; it was just hammer, hammer, hammer. I didn't fare much better at that job either; one had to be fast to earn good money and after two weeks I was reluctantly sacked.

'Sorry, son, we need fast workers; you're taking up valuable bench space and I've people waiting for jobs.'

May 1947; unemployed. So I went back to the morning and evening paper rounds, and spent any sunny days in Brentwood open air swimming pool, often with George, who had now left school and was looking for his first job. During this period I took great pleasure in doing the housework for Mum. I quite liked making beds, sweeping up, and making the kitchen sink shine. I'd seen Dad many a time use the fine, grey ashes from the fire grate to clean the cutlery and the sink; ashes were good for getting stains off; no fancy scouring powder had appeared in our household as yet. Mum's face was a picture when she came in from work and saw her house all spick and span.

"The Biggest Van in Essex" was painted in large letters down the full length of the furniture van. It *was* big too, as big as a house, or so it seemed to me that first morning I reported for work as a van boy.

'You're our guard dog, son,' said the driver. 'Whenever we are working you never leave the back of the van. No pinching that way, see?' No I didn't see, but I wasn't going to argue. A job was a job and the money wasn't bad. Summer had arrived and what could be better than life on the open road?

The van worked out of an alleyway next to the Maypole in Brentwood High Street and, unfortunately, only two shops away from Mr and Mrs Bell. Still, I reasoned, they won't see me if I'm in the van.

The driver and his two mates were very happy guys and we got on well. We plied our trade up and down the arterial road, and worked anywhere from Ilford to Southend. Many times it was early starts, six in the morning, and late finishes but they always gave me a share of the tips. I understood what the driver had meant about guard dog when I saw the back of the van; it had no doors, just a tailboard with a sheet of canvas above it, which was normally rolled up and tied at roof level. The tail-board was two feet six inches high and a rope dropped from the rolled canvas down to its centre. One yank and the canvas unrolled.

My job was to sit in the back of the van at all times and I watched the world go by as I gazed out over dusty roads, built-up areas and fuming traffic, but mostly green fields and lovely countryside. Only when it was raining did the driver and his mates tell me to drop the canvas; then I would poke my head around the side of it and think my own thoughts.

It was a carefree two months that I spent, carrying furniture in and out of houses, sitting in transport cafés having a good fry-up, or rumbling along in the back of the van in my own world, dreaming my dreams.

When we arrived at a house it was already stripped and packed into many and various boxes and cardboard cartons of all sizes; the householder was responsible for packing everything. Many times it was poorly packed and rarely was it labelled. Time was always against us as the firm's motto was "There and back in a day."

Our territory from Southend to Ilford meant we could pick up early in the morning and deliver the same day, even on the longest journey, but it also meant many early starts and late finishes, even though people didn't have as much furniture then as they do today.

We were emptying a house in Rayleigh as the widow woman was moving to the coast at Westcliffe-on-Sea. Once she'd spoken to the driver she said she was going to say her goodbyes to the neighbours and left us to it.

We set to with a will; the quicker we loaded up, the more time we got in the cafés. We soon had the house empty and the old lady returned.

'Where's Joey?' she cried, her face wrinkling anxiously.

'Joey who?' said Bill the driver.

'My budgie, Joey, what have you done with him?'

'I ain't seen no budgie missus. Have you?' he asked, glancing over his shoulder at me and Harry. We shook our heads.

'I put his cage in a cardboard box. He was coming with me.' She was almost on the brink of tears.

'Must be in the van then,' said Bill. 'We'll see he gets there all right.'

There had been dozens of cardboard boxes, most of which I'd carried into the van. They were all stacked at the back, with beds, sideboards, tables, chairs and all the big stuff around them. The old girl wanted Bill to unload the van, but he wouldn't.

'He'll be all right with us, missus; we'll have him out soon as we get there.'

Then the poor old girl *did* cry but time was passing. We left and I felt sorry for her. I tried to look through the piled up furniture for a right sized box that might hold the bird but it was impossible. We trundled along to a transport café and I listened for bird noises when the engine stopped in the car park; not a sound. It's dead, I thought.

Bill and Harry thought it was a great joke as they wolfed the bacon, sausage and eggs. I sat sipping my tea and willing them to get a move on so that we could resurrect the bird.

The widow woman was waiting at her new bungalow when we got there and stood nervously watching the back of the van as the big furniture was unloaded. She sprang into action as soon as the boxes came into sight. She found energy she never knew she had as she went up the wooden ramp like a steeple chaser. I was at her side.

'That one,' she said, pointing. Oh heck, I thought, it would be the bottom one.

We extracted the bottom box and quickly moved down the ramp. She placed it on the roadside and fumbled with the loose string. The three of us stood watching, waiting for the tragedy to unfold. She pulled the cage from the cardboard box and, as daylight hit it, Joey jumped from the bottom of the cage, on to his perch, and started tweeting. The old lady laughed to relieve her tension and fear and, with tears running down her face, mumbled endearments as she kissed the cage near Joey's perch. All three of us were wreathed in smiles.

'There, I told you, missus. He enjoyed that little ride,' said Bill.

Mum had never been happy that I was working on the removal van; she thought it was dangerous travelling the roads, but I convinced her with my enthusiasm that everything would be all right. The early morning start was acceptable but she was worried from tea-time onwards until I arrived home, sometimes at nine or ten o'clock at night.

The night I didn't arrive, I knew she wouldn't let me go back.

The day came when we picked up a job from Ilford and it took a long time to load. It was nearly two in the afternoon before we left. With our stop for late lunch we didn't get to Southend until seven at night. It was then the end of July so it stayed light until ten or after. By nine o'clock we were unloaded and on our way back. But the ritual of pulling into a transport café for a meal still had to be observed even at that time of night.

When we'd eaten I went for a pee and then I sat on the back of the van, legs dangling, waiting for the others to come back. It was always my job to put up the tailboard before we left but I usually waited until they came.

I was sitting there day dreaming when—suddenly—the engine burst into life and the van took a great lurch forward. I shot off the back like a lump of wet soap squeezed in your hand and landed on my face, in clouds of dust. The rough unmade car park claimed the skin of my nose, left cheek and both hands and knees. I lay there bleeding as the dust settled on me and the van disappeared into the night.

It came out later that Bill and Harry were already in the driving cab when I came back from having a pee. They saw me coming back and assumed everything was fine. Bill reckoned his foot slipped off the clutch as he started the engine; he said he could remember them laughing and Harry saying, 'That'll wake Bob up.'

They only missed me after they realised that the van was making more noise than usual and, after ten minutes driving, they stopped to check and found the tailboard down and me missing. By the time they returned to the café I'd been taken to Southend Hospital, patched up and was on my way home in an ambulance. For Mum that was the end.

'I knew something would happen; you're not going back there anymore.' So I convalesced at home, all scabby and sore.

Father had something to say when he came home that weekend. It seemed that I was the one who was always in trouble. Vic got on all right on the buildings, Ernie was studying hard and getting good results at school. Pauline was no problem and never got into any trouble or caused any concern. Had God made me different? I wondered.

'Just how many jobs have you had now, son?' asked Father in serious mood.

'Don't know, Dad,' I said, feeling the third degree coming on.

'At least seven, I would think, in just a year,' Father mused more to himself than to me. 'What you want is a trade, maybe an apprenticeship. I'm home for a week so we will have a hunt around.'

True to his word, the next week we ended up again in front of Misery Guts in the Labour Exchange. Home from Home, I thought.

'Trainee, not exactly an apprenticeship, but he will learn how to become an expert upholsterer if he sticks it,' said Misery Guts to Father.

'Well, it's worth a try. I'll take him along; thank you for your help,' and Father took the proffered paper-slip and left.

The upholsterer's was a two-man, back street business, operating out of a big wooden shed behind the pub at the very bottom of Brentwood High Street. There was a funeral parlour on the opposite corner. The shed was full of old sofas and armchairs, with a space in the middle where skeletons of previously happy armchairs were waiting for new flesh to be put on their wooden bones.

'We don't make new furniture. No wood about, you see. We repair and refurbish old suites,' said the owner to Dad. 'Only started the business last year when we came out the Forces but it's going well; that's why we need a boy.'

Dad talked to him about the work, hours and money.

'Of course,' said the man, 'we'll teach him the trade from the bottom up, have no fear.'

So I started, job number eight, I think, and the best of it was I was only a minute from Harry's café and Harry was delighted to see me back.

It was now August and my days were spent breathing generations of filthy dust as I stripped down settees and armchairs of their cracked leather, dirty moquette and filthy horsehair. I was taking their guts out, denuding them, leaving them cold and stark and threatened. Old frames had to be strengthened, joints remade, wood replaced, but not by me. I was the boy, I made the tea,

167

fetched this, delivered that, swept up a mess here, and tore the guts out of a stinking chair there. Two weeks slipped into four. The owner taught me nothing yet he'd promised Father everything. I had a go at him and we argued.

'Everybody has to start at the bottom,' he said. 'When you prove yourself we'll start teaching you the trade.'

Prove myself, what the hell was he on about?

I continued eating dust and doing all the shitty jobs; I had no choice as I saw it. If I left my job again Dad would give up on me and I didn't want to cause Mum any more worry. By September I could hardly stand it any longer.

I lay in bed thinking what I could do and for the first time realised that you didn't have to be out of a job to look for another. What a revelation that was. I sat up in bed and shouted, 'Yippee!'

'You daft or something? Get off to sleep,' said big brother Vic. I lay there smiling to myself and planning my next move.

The next few lunches I had a quick fried egg sandwich in Harry's and then nipped down the thirty yards to the Labour Exchange. At first Misery Guts thought I'd left my job. I put him right but when I explained my plan to find a new job before I left the present one, he was not impressed at all; his face never changed expression.

'Be thankful for what you've got, son. There aren't any more jobs.' Three days running I plucked up courage to approach the miserable sod again. 'Are you sure there are no jobs, sir?'

'Don't waste my time, son, go away.' Sod you, too, I thought.

The third day I was leaving the counter and crossing the drab, unpolished linoleum when I noticed a new poster on the wall. It was a very colourful poster and quite large. In the centre of the blue background was a graceful Spitfire blazing a trail through the sky. Below it was a picture of an innocent-looking boy dressed in RAF uniform wearing a forage cap at a smart angle. He looked just like me. Underneath the boy, in big letters, it said, "Boys fifteen years to sixteen years may apply now to join the Royal Air Force." I gasped; it looked beautiful, exciting even; fancy learning all about Spitfires. I went back to the counter, all bright-eyed, keen even.

'Could I join the Royal Air Force?'

Christ, I didn't believe it, Misery Guts was smiling! I expected his face to fall into pieces at any moment.

'Course you can, son, if your Mum and Dad will fill in this

168

form and sign it,' he said beaming.

He obviously realised that this was his great opportunity to remove the thorn from his side that had been giving him pain for the last fourteen months. I clutched the form excitedly as I left and couldn't wait for knocking-off time so I could go home and get Mum to fill it in.

'Oh, I don't know, Bob. You don't want to leave us again, do you?' she said.

'But, Mum, it's different. I can come home every weekend and I'm older now,' I told her, totally misguided as ever, and full of the romanticism conjured up by the poster in my still innocent mind. Mum laid the form on the sideboard. 'Your Dad will be home at the weekend; we'll see what he says.'

For all the joy of Civvy Street and the untold pleasure and security of being back with my family, there were still times when I felt different from the rest of my brothers. The five years in the Dukies had somehow changed me. I was looking back now and seeing good things. You remember them more often than you remember the bad. That indefinable sense of belonging to a group of friends, all in the same boat, all facing the same hardship, no-one better off than anyone else and all prepared to fight for their mates. The comradeship and true deep friendships were missing in civvy street. Neither my brothers or George and Alan could fill the gap that was as pronounced now, after fourteen months out of the Dukies, as it had ever been.

I used to daydream about Cockney Alf and try to imagine what he would be doing at the farm and what Joe would be doing at the school. I was now fifteen years and nine months old, and if one added together all the time I'd ever spent with my mother it came to just over one year in Worcester and one year four months in Brentwood. India didn't really count as the ayahs spent more time with us than our mothers or fathers did.

I'd had no contact at all with girls; in fact, I don't think I really recognised they existed until I saw Jill's brown flannel knickers. Neither the Dukies schooling, or Father and Mother had mentioned anything about sex, nor did they ever. I was wordly-wise in some ways but totally naive in many others. Although happy in my home life I felt something was missing. I didn't know where I was going, I had no direction in life, no goal at all and I felt very unsettled.

Dad came home that weekend; it was a turning-point in the

169

lives of the Freeman children. Not only did I want to join the RAF as a Boy Entrant; Victor wanted to join the Army.

Vic was nearly eighteen years old and was into sport and physical fitness; he was also playing in a band. I would think that Dad was delighted that his eldest son wanted to follow in his footsteps; but as for me wanting to join the Royal Air Force—that was something entirely different.

Mum and Dad stayed up talking into the night. I lay in bed straining my ears to catch the conversation. Mother didn't want me to go and she pleaded with Father as only as mother can. Dad could see further than emotion.

'The boy needs a trade,' he said. 'Look at the jobs he's had; he'll never make his way in civvy street; the Forces will make a man of him.' Poor Mother couldn't win.

On the 14th October 1947, Father took me for tests, interviews and a medical examination to the RAF Station at North Weald, Essex.

Before I went to sleep that night I was signed, sealed and delivered into what was only the second intake of Boy Entrants since the end of the war.

For someone who hated authority and unfairness, whose temper and obstinate nature had already fashioned his life, entry into the Royal Air Force could promise little but disaster and unhappiness. Yet I could see no further than the beautiful, graceful Spitfire on the poster which conjured up an image of excitement and glamour.

My dream was to have a wonderful future as a Brylcreem Boy, with every unspoken hope and wish for the future fulfilled.

The reality was to turn out to be something very different.

Bob Freeman's True Story
continues in

THE BRYLCREEM BOY
*with frequent battles against mindless
authority and seas of bullshit*

This is how it really was.
A lot of laughs, great mates and
some very hard times in the Royal Air Force.

From all good booksellers or direct from the publisher.